TAIMAK

THE LAST DRAGON

AN AUTOBIOGRAPHY

For more information, to inquire about rights to this or other works, or to

purchase copies for special educational, business, or sales promotional uses please write to:

Incorgnito Publishing Press
A division of Market Management Group, LLC
33 S. Wilson Avenue, Suite 113
Pasadena, California 91106

FIRST EDITION

Printed in the United States of America

ISBN: 978-1-944589-04-2

10 9 8 7 6 5 4 3 2 1

To my mother and father,

to all my fans,

to all dedicated artists,

and everyone that has the courage to go beyond their limitations of right and wrong

and make this world a more peaceful, safe and exciting place.

Prologue – The Race of Life

However you look at it, there will always be a mountain in front of you. When you try to do something big, you're gonna face obstacles and challenges - there's always going to be someone who is faster, stronger, more skilled. Your fiercest challenger might even be yourself; all of your doubts, insecurities, and anxieties whirling around inside of you are usually the toughest obstacles that you need to overcome. Alright, I know that sounds like a cheesy line you've heard a million times before, but maaaan...I've lived it and I know it's true!

I remember a moment that was especially tough. It was the second time that I ran the epic, exhausting, stomach-churnin' New York City Marathon. Like most challenges, a really intense marathon is as much psychological and emotional as it is physical. I learned that the first time I ran one. This time, however, was going to completely push me to the limit of what I could do.

My friend Willy and I had put in the work to train our butts off, and we were ready. We headed up to the starting line in Staten Island, feeling loose and confident. When the gun went off, we immediately fell into our running rhythm. After a little while, Willy fell behind; he was older than me and he knew that he had to hang back, even though he was still in amazing shape. I kept pressing on, and pretty soon I was in the zone.

I was out on my own and feeling good. I caught up to another runner who was keeping a pretty fast pace. We chatted and he asked me whether I had run the marathon before. I said yes and then he told me to stick with him if I wanted to beat my previous record of 3 hours and 20 minutes. I didn't know what I was getting into, but I was up for a challenge, of course, and I love to learn from people who are able to help me grow. Help me beat my time? "I'm with you...let's do this!"

At first, it seemed like I had total triumph right in the palm of my hands! As my feet pounded against the concrete and I hurtled through the city streets, I felt like my body was a fist, punching into an opponent's chest. I let that energy carry me forward, riding on a wave of momentum. It was like I was going to win a fight! But if the race was my opponent, it was about to fight back. I looked over at my running partner and asked him, "What time are you trying to beat?" He said that he had run many marathons and the previous year, he came in at 2 hours and 28 minutes. This year, he wanted to get in at 2 hours and 20 minutes. I was impressed. Even after running for quite a while, his pace still looked good.

All of a sudden, I felt like I had run right into a brick building and started slowing down. This was the infamous runner's wall that I had always heard about. My racing buddy looked as smooth and strong as ever, but I was totally sapped. We had been running a 5.5 minute mile pace, (which is much faster than I was used to) and my legs just couldn't keep it up. It was like the life had been sucked out of me. My new pal wished me luck and kept trucking on without me.

It was a lonely feeling. My legs were like stones and my feet were like clumps of clay. I saw the Queensboro Bridge in the distance, and it seemed like a looming mountain. I had only run twelve miles, and there was still a lot of race to go. I told myself, this is it, this is what it takes, dig in, it's all in your mind, Taimak, no matter what you feel - it's all in your mind. *Keep going.*

There was no easy way to finish. I couldn't pack my bags and move to a different neighborhood; I couldn't change my phone number; I couldn't lie on my resume; I couldn't take some magic pill. This was raw and simple, my feet in sneakers hitting the concrete. It hurt, and if I wanted to finish, it was going to hurt some more. That's how life is, though. Nothing about life is easy, and I've had such a crazy, lucky, tough, challenging road to get to where I am today. There were times where it hurt like hell, where my legs or my arms or my brain or my heart gave out, and I just didn't think that I could go on. But I had to keep going!

I slowed down a bit, but I kept running and talking to myself. "Come on Taimak, here's the wall, now go through it, breathe and keep going". I don't like starting things without finishing them and this had to get done. I said I was going to finish the race faster and I would! I kept running, I looked at the Queensboro Bridge and I said to my completely drained legs, "We're going to do this, you guys listen to me. We have around 10-12 miles to go and you're going to keep running until you cross the finish line".

And that's what I did; I went over the bridge. It was carpeted, which was better than running on metal or cement, but it was still a hard surface so I did my best not to pound my feet and to absorb the impact by bending my knees. When I got over the bridge and started going uptown on 1st Avenue, people were screaming, "Keep going!" It was inspiring. I didn't give my mind an opportunity to think negatively, I kept pressing on and going through Spanish Harlem - Salsa music playing, screams of "Boricua!!" – and then on into Harlem.

Someone shouted from the crowd of well-wishers: "On my God, is that Taimak? Keep going, Bruce Leroy!" I didn't have the energy to do anything but nod in appreciation. Once I got to 5th Avenue and saw the park, I knew there wasn't too much left in me. At the same time, every mile felt more like 5 miles. At every step, people were watching all of us runners; some people were screaming, some looking over in admiration, some thinking we were just crazy. But for me, at this point there wasn't much thinking about anything else, except finishing as strong as I could. I made the turn on 59th Street alongside Central Park south towards the final stage, the entrance into the Park to the finish line: *feet don't fail me now.* Turning into the park I felt a rush of finality; I made it! Only a little more, come on, let's do it! I picked up my pace and began to run as fast as I could and heard the grateful support of the spectators as they cheered us all on. I made it past the finish line.

In this book, I'm going to talk about my life and my many experiences: with martial arts, with films, with my family, with women, and with my fans. I'm going to talk about the race that I've been running, and about the difficulties that I've overcome that have almost stopped me from finishing. It's been a true marathon, with triumphs and setbacks, pains and pleasures. In the end, it's a story of hope and accomplishing your dreams, believing in yourself and pushing yourself to the limit so that you can achieve everything that you want.

This autobiography also contains some of my creative work, including poems and excerpts from two of my screenplays, which are titled *I've Seen Things* and *The Professor*. In *I've Seen Things*, I play a detective named Ray Larson who gets caught up in a deadly, seductive mystery. In *The Professor*, I play Frank Carter, a college philosophy professor with a dark past. I've placed these creative works at particular points in my story, and I'd like you to see these poems and scenes as reflections of the emotions I felt at different points in my life. You'll also find a special bonus at the end of the manuscript. I collaborated with screenwriter Danny MacDonald to write an original treatment for a sequel to *The Last Dragon* called *The Last Dragon: Guardians of the Glow*. A treatment is basically a summary of a movie that you create before you write a full-length screenplay. When you read this treatment, it will be sort of like reading a short story. I hope that you enjoy diving back into the adventures of Bruce Leroy, right from the mind of Bruce Leroy himself!

Chapter 1 – Beginnings

"The gain is not the having of children; it is the discovery of love and how to be loving."

Polly Berrien Berends

Before you finish a race, you need to take your first steps across the starting line. I began my race in 1964: I was born in Los Angeles, the son of a mixed race couple (my mother is African-American and my father is of Italian descent). My parents were and are incredibly creative, passionate people, and I'd like to begin my own story by talking about my parents and their lives. Once you learn a bit about them, you'll be able understand where I come from and how I got to be the Taimak that I am today (oh, and for the record, it's Tie-mock, not Tie-mack).

My father, Cosmo Guarriello, was a singer, and he began his singing career like a lot of nice Italian boys of the times, as a choir boy at church. When he got older, he took his talents to downtown New York City to entertain crowds, working with his close friend Raymond Fleming. They sang the popular tunes of the time to entertain the passersby, hoping for the occasional nickel that might come their way. Raymond had a friend in the music business, a talent scout; he introduced this scout to my father and he eventually took my father to meet a producer named Bobby Robinson of the Fire and Fury record label.

Robinson was looking for an act to compete with Frankie Avalon and Fabian, who were very popular at the time. For his audition with Robinson, my father sang "Chances Are", which had been made popular by Johnny Mathis. Robinson was so impressed that he signed my father to a contract right away and recorded him with a thirteen piece orchestra! My father was only eighteen years-old when he signed that deal!

Although things didn't move as well as he would've wished, my father was noticed by song writer/producer Teddy Vann, who decided to buy out his contract from Robinson. Vann wanted to record my father singing a song called "Teenager for President". This was during the time that John F. Kennedy and Richard Nixon were competing for the presidency. Vann thought it would be a great marketing idea to promote my father as a teenager for president. The song was an immediate hit and made it to the Billboard Top 100 Songs in the country. My father changed his name to Tony Cosmo and then appeared on shows like American Bandstand and became an instant success.

Unfortunately, this was the 1950's and the height of the payola scandals. Payola in radio was the act of record producers paying DJs to play a certain song. This meant that they were buying access to the radio station audience without labeling the "play" of the song as an advertisement. Some big names were involved in the scandal including Dick Clark. Roulette Records, the label producing "Teenager for President", was taking advantage of the practice as well. Once the scandal was made public and those involved were investigated, the jig was up. This put a damper on my father's song and "Teenager for President" never climbed to the top spot on the charts as it might have done.

My father also recorded other songs written and produced by Vann Records, such as "The Big Party" and "Tiny Hands and Funny Dimples," and he also recorded "Pony Tail Annie and Crew Cut Joe" and "Wise To You" for Fling Records. After that short stint in Hollywood and the recording world, Tony Cosmo decided that show business just wasn't for him. I think that my dad was a bit embarrassed by the whole thing. He didn't really tell me about his singing career until I was much older, and I didn't find out any specific details until I wrote this book. He really only thought that "Teenager for President" was a good song and he didn't like the others that the company had him sing: he didn't think that they were soulful or strong enough.

My father was born in the Bronx, a second generation Italian-American. His grandparents were from a little town outside of Naples, Italy called Benevento. His father was born in New York but he returned to the family town of Benevento to meet a wife. With his mission accomplished, he returned to New York's Italian Harlem with his new wife who was now pregnant with my father.

Growing up in an extremely traditional Italian family it was pre-determined that my father would marry a nice Italian girl. But that wasn't going to happen, because my father was crazy about black women and black culture. My father spent a lot of time downtown, hanging out at a club called The Port of Call.

My mother Laurita grew up in Harlem, New York and worked at the Apollo Theatre. She was really close with, and in some cases grew up with, people like Jackie Wilson, Jimi Hendrix, James Brown and a number of other young celebrities. She also knew Leonard Reed, who would become one of my father's music producers and Bobby Schiffman, who ran the Apollo from 1960 until 1976. Bobby famously said, "For years, you could write *Apollo Theater* on a postcard, drop it into a mailbox anywhere, and it would be delivered. How many theaters can you say that about?" Schiffman always claimed that the Apollo was a mix of romance and reality. "When you stepped on that stage," said Otis Williams of The Temptations, "you knew who'd been there before."

My mother had two boys, Lance and Sharif, from a previous marriage with a gangster and boxer named Donald Hayes. He was part of an infamous group of brothers called the Hayes brothers, who ran Harlem in the 1960's. When my mother met my father, Donald was actually in prison for armed robbery. My parents met in Greenwich Village, in downtown Manhattan at The Port of Call; it was the New York "in" spot for artists and a real hub of creativity. They fell in love almost instantly as a friend of my mother's recalled. She told me, "Your mother fell in love with him before he even noticed her. Every night, she would get dressed to the nines and go to that club just in the hopes that she would catch his eye." Eventually, he did notice her and their romance began. They were very young when they got together – he was 19 and she was 23.

When my father abruptly left for Hollywood and fame, my mother would have none of that separation. She was still enamored with my father and determined to be with him, so she moved to Hollywood to join him shortly before he quit his entertainment career. They lived there for about two years and had two children during that time. My brother, Meishan, was their firstborn, in 1962, and I was born two years later, in 1964. I was born in the Year of the Dragon, just like Bruce Lee…sounds like destiny, right?

My father's family was close-knit and nice, but like most people at the time, they were still ignorant when it came to race. However, that didn't affect my parents too much. They ran with a relatively more progressive and artistic group of friends, so the prejudice they experienced wasn't so bad on the east coast. In California, however, they dealt with a level of prejudice that they weren't used to. For instance, my mother had to stay in the car when they looked for an apartment, because there was the possibility that they might be shunned by the renter.

My father borrowed some money from his parents to open a second hand antique store in Hollywood. My parents lived in the store itself, in a small room in the back, where my mother would cook collard greens and other soul food specialties on the hot radiator. They had a small, full-size bed in the room and would hang their clothes all around the room because there wasn't any closet space. My father had pretty decent success with selling antiques; he is a very artistic person and he taught himself how to restore furniture. He didn't necessarily inherit that artistry and creativity from his family.

His grandfather, for instance, had more conventional professions, like owning a bakery and working in a bank.

One trait my father did inherit from his parents was his natural good looks and physique. My dad was a great-looking guy and women were always after him. Even as a boy and teen, the girls would talk about how good looking he was. He was often bullied in his neighborhood, even by his friends; they didn't like that the girls liked him so much. Dad would have fought back, but his father never taught him how. Though my grandfather actually used to box, he didn't want to teach my father to be a violent person. My grandfather reasoned that when someone knows how to fight, they won't back down and that will lead to even more fighting.

My father knew that women were crazy about him and he liked to take advantage of his good looks. When he worked on the antique furniture outside of his store, he would be deliberately shirtless. My mother told me that rich women drove by and stopped to proposition him. One such woman was a famous actress, Joan Blondell who was known for movie roles in the 30's and 40's (though she worked in television up until her death in 1979). She bought some stuff from my father's antique store and had him personally bring it to her house. She made passes at my dad but he just wasn't attracted to her.

Still, my dad was a 20 year-old Italian stud dealing with the temptations of the Hollywood scene, and living with a pregnant black woman in, what was unfortunately, a racist town. All of this proved to be too much for him, and not all of the propositions went unanswered. But it was especially challenging for my mother. She was young and pregnant with my brother Meishan. Unfortunately, sometimes my mother and father were like oil and water and they argued a lot. It finally got so bad that they had to break up.

My mother didn't have any money and she had no place to go. It was a very hard time for her, to say the least. There was a government housing program for single pregnant women back then. When couples had domestic problems, the government would provide the woman with a place to live, a room in someone else's house. My mother was sent to a town that was a bit away from Hollywood. She stayed with a white couple in a town that was entirely white; it became clear that most of the townspeople had never even seen a black person. The people that my mother was staying with were certainly very nice, but their friends would come by the house and awkwardly stare at her. She obviously didn't feel comfortable when she was around these guests. It was challenging for my mother on many levels and although she didn't want to call my father for a long time, she eventually did. He finally came to get her and they reunited. I was born soon afterwards.

After a two year stint in Hollywood and just a few months after I was born, my parents decided to move back to New York. New York is where I have my first solid memories, and I'll always remember it as the place where my spirit really came alive. If Los Angeles was where I took my first steps as a baby, New York was where I really learned how to run the race of life and where I learned how to be a passionate, intense, and eager participant in this great big, crazy marathon of existence. I owe a lot to my parents, who showed me beauty and what it meant to be excited and passionate about life.

In New York my parents were a young bohemian couple. They ran with the hip, cool, creative "in" crowd. They constantly hosted parties and we always had a good time, dancing and listening to good music. They were friends with many talented artists and celebrities like Iggy Pop, Andy Warhol, Candy Darling, Liza Minelli, Geraldo Rivera, and the actor Calvin Lockhart, who was like an uncle to me. He had such a great sense of humor! When my parents threw a party, every hipster in New York wanted to be there to join in on the fun. There weren't only celebrities at these gatherings, though. I remember my uncle Jason (he was a family friend, not my biological uncle) and his boisterous laugh – he was tall and dark skinned, a singer/model, and a fun guy with a charismatic personality. People really loved him. He was a wonderful gay man - or, at least, I thought he was, until he later fell in love with a blonde Englishwoman named Margot.

My mother Laurita had this powerful ability to attract people. She was famous for her talents in the kitchen; she cooked food for the gods, and her specialty was her delicious soul food. Later on, when we moved to London, she even opened the first soul food restaurant in the city, second in all of Europe, called Laurita's. She wasn't only known for her food… she was a natural psychic and gave quite accurate readings under the name Laurita Cosmos. She read for many celebrities and their friends. For instance, she gave readings to the extraordinarily talented photographer, Francesco Scavullo, as well as the internationally known British rock band The New Seekers, just after their first appearance on *The Ed Sullivan Show*.

There was this high profile, private, under the radar club in New York back in the 60's called The Auxpuce Café on 55th off of Park

Avenue. My mother and father went there all the time. One night, they were waiting to get in when Ed Sullivan came to the door and saw them - or rather, he saw my mother. He was immediately taken by her and asked her name and then invited her and my father to come inside with him. He was extremely personal and acted like he knew her for years and then he introduced her to many of the high rollers there.

That's the type of magnetism that she has always had with people. Being accepted at the Auxpuce meant she also got access to another legendary star, Judy Garland. Judy was sitting down having dinner one night when she called my mother over and introduced herself. Judy wanted my mother to give her a psychic reading. My mother doesn't like to give dark or sinister information in her readings. She will only, at most, warn her clients about something that they should avoid. During her reading of Judy, my mother picked up that she was getting ready to go to London and there was something else as well...something dark. She warned Judy that it wouldn't be good to go to London at that time, but Judy said that was ridiculous. She had to be there, and there was no way that she wasn't going to go. Not too long after my mother's reading, Judy went to London and died of a drug overdose in Chelsea.

Because my father was such a great performer and my mother had such a magnetic, bohemian spirit, they were surrounded by artistic friends and they were always involved in artistic spectacles. An especially creative night happened in 1969 or so, when my father conceived of and organized an extravagant event called "The Everything Is Everything Costume Ball," which was co-financed by Roy Hayes, the brother of my mom's ex-husband. Ticket sales were low and my mother realized that she needed to find a way to get the word out on a large scale. She called her friend, the famous newscaster Geraldo Rivera. He took an ABC news crew over to my parents' place so that he could interview her about the event. While my mom and dad pitched the event, my uncle Jason and a few of his friends danced in the background, wearing amazing costumes. Needless to say, people got interested and the event was a huge success; it was attended by the most influential and hip people in Manhattan.

Hundreds of people attended in extremely ornate and creative costumes. This was no run of the mill masquerade party. There was a contest for the best costume, and these costumes were creative and, in most cases, quite elaborate. Meishan got to announce the contest winner: a young man who came as "The Tree of Life." He wore a sparkling white outfit and he balanced a white, self-made, shimmering "tree" on his head, shoulders, and arms. It was at least 20 feet tall! To top it all off my parents got married during the ball – by a very drunk Santa Claus.

Through all of the ups and downs of my parents' relationship, there remains one constant thing: a passionate love for creativity. I was always surrounded by artists, art, and creative expression. My parents had so many artistic friends and they were always involved in unique projects, which opened up my eyes to a whole world of creativity and performance. Everyone was kind, creative, interesting, exciting and beautiful. I don't think that there was ever one boring person around my parents.

Inspired by all of this creativity, I quickly grew to love performing. My mother said that out of all of her children, I began walking the earliest and I had an immediate love for dancing. When I was 4 or 5 years old, I loved to dance for my relatives. I was good at it, and they enjoyed it and thought it was great fun. They always had me do the Funky Chicken and the James Brown shuffle. I was quickly becoming used to performing, even at this young age. While I was a toddler, my mother took me to an audition for a Vaseline commercial. She was worried about the chances of me getting the job because I had recently crawled onto a heated grill that was lying on the floor, causing me to burn my butt. She said she was elated when they apparently didn't care at all about the burn marks. They had just fallen in love with me and my personality and I got the commercial.

Aside from my early passion for performing, my youthful years were also filled with lots of love and family. I have two younger sisters, Naria and Taiesha, and I was around 6 years old when Naria was born. I was completely enamored to have a little girl in our family, my mother's first daughter. When she was born, I was ecstatic and couldn't stop kissing her. It was like having a new doll or something. She had golden hair - her own daughter, Gianna, now has the same golden hair. Gianna's hair is a little less curly, but she's just as adorable. I also had two half-brothers, my mother's sons from her first marriage. They lived with their paternal grandparents, and we visited with them quite often. I can dimly recall my own grandfather, who died when I was very young. I remember him taking me to the movies and looking at me with a beautiful smile. I also remember my three aunts, Yvonne, Gail and Paula, who were all very sweet and loving ladies.

My childhood memories aren't only about creativity and family love, though. I got bad beatings from a babysitter who we called Aunt Ethel (though she wasn't my biological aunt). My brother and I used to stay over at her place along with what I believe were her teenage daughters. Aunt Ethel used to babysit a whole group of kids. We all became so nervous and afraid whenever she came home from work. It was as though she came home for one purpose: to beat us. I'd run away, trying to hide and find refuge. I used to hide under the bed and when she found me there, she would drag me out from under the bed and beat with me with a wire hanger, her weapon of choice for us. I was so scared that I would pee on myself. These days, I feel complete and resolved about what went down back then. However, I remember experiencing real fear as a child. It was a terrifying ordeal to go through as a kid. On one occasion, all of us were watching *The Wizard of Oz* on TV and we were introduced to the Wicked Witch of the West. After seeing that movie, I couldn't help imagining that Aunt Ethel was the Wicked Witch. She wore a dark, corporate-style suit to work, and when she came home, it was really as if the Wicked Witch had just walked through the door.

Unfortunately, my mother also participated in the practice of child beating. For her, it was discipline...but to me, as a child, it was a violent beating, and it filled me with fear. She often did it with the belt or an electrical cord. I recognize that this is an accepted part of many cultures and I know that there was a different attitude about this issue in the 1970's, but it definitely had a very negative effect on me as a child. I eventually developed a problem with wetting the bed and I couldn't stop. I don't know if the beatings were the cause of it or if it was other psychological problems, but it was not an easy time for me. My mother didn't mean for her beatings to have such a bad effect on me. I know that she was trying to discipline me and not to abuse me. Aunt Ethel, on the other hand, took some sort of sadistic joy in what she was doing. My parents tried to help me stop the bedwetting without realizing that their harsh punishments and my babysitter's violent thrashings were probably the cause of my problems. I didn't know how to properly communicate with them. My parents bought me a padded sheet that would give a minor electrical shock whenever I wet the sheets. It would wake me up in the middle of night to teach me to go to the bathroom. It didn't really work, but I was fortunately able to grow out of this problem by the time I was about 8 years old. However, I still had other side effects from the beatings that I suffered. I had severe earaches, and my mother used to put warm essential oils in my ears and massage my head to comfort me.

As time wore on, my parents' marriage began to deteriorate. They were both very young and, at the time, the pressure of an interracial marriage and raising four children was just too difficult. Unfortunately, sometimes my mother and father would clash in a very dramatic way, and I remember them fighting a lot. I never knew what they were fighting about because I was very young, but I can remember it happening as far back as when I was 4 years-old. Once, my father even grabbed my tricycle and lifted it up, threatening my mother during an argument. I remember jumping up and grabbing the wheel of the bicycle, trying to pull it back down. My father was very young and he didn't know how to deal with my mother, who wouldn't back down to him and didn't hold back her loud, determined opinions.

As you can see, I had a very tumultuous and intense childhood. Those early years gave me my passion for creativity and my love of performing, which has been with me ever since. I learned a lot about life: that education wasn't always easy, but it was always unique, and it prepared me for the long and exciting race ahead.

Rumble

Run run no no I'll be good, please don't please...

He doesn't know he's 6 years-old he doesn't know....

Where's my belt the leather strap wrapped tight
around her wrist...

Where's my belt....no please noooo...

She can't find the belt, buying time, time...

Pulling the extension cord from the wall, make it
quick, please make it quick!

But on the bedroom floor is a wire hanger, pulled
apart to teach this child a lesson a lesson...

Screams echo in the background of children playing
in the playground,

Screams echo in the background of children playing
in the playground

As he hides under the couch urine streaming
down his pants...

WHAT...WERE...YOU...DOING?

Whip...screams echo in the background of children
playing in the playground...

Whip...screams echo in the background of children
playing in the playground.

Will he find a hero? Will he find a hero? Will he be
free?

Screams from his naked skin, welts left from the
whips, the wire hanger an option only the lowest
criminals deserve to feel...

Mommy!!!!! I love you, Mommy.

Screams echo in the background of children playing
in the playground,

Will he find a hero? Will he be free?

Chapter 2 – Adventures in Europe (A Breath of Fresh Air)

I wish you bluebirds in the spring

To give your heart a song to sing

And then a kiss, but more than this

I wish you love

From the American remake of a French song,
"Que reste-t-il de nos amours?"

When I was about 7 years-old, my mom persuaded my dad to leave the U.S. and move to London. Her friends kept telling her how wonderful life was there and that the racial aspects of life for black folks were much less severe. My dad wanted to continue to do the costume balls back in New York, but he eventually caved in to her demands. So, we all moved to London - my mom, dad, two sisters, my brother and me.

To me, Europe felt like being reborn. I was just a kid from New York, and all of a sudden I realized that there was this completely different way of life. When I was in New York, I was surrounded by traffic, horns blaring, and concrete streets, but now I was immersed in ancient history and a new kind of culture. My brother and I went to a school in Chelsea called Park Walk Primary School. Although we were new to the school and didn't know anybody there, Meishan made friends pretty quickly. He was 9 and more mature than I was, and he was definitely the smartest kid in school. He also had an innate leadership quality and other kids would follow him; he created his own clique of about five different buddies.

Despite being Meishan's little brother, I wasn't considered part of the cool crowd. Whenever Meishan was with his friends, they would all pick on me. It used to infuriate me. Eventually, the bullying really got to me. The fury in me kept building up until I cornered a couple of my brother's friends when they were by themselves. I beat them up in retaliation for everything that they had done to me. I didn't feel bad about it, though, because they had really made me suffer.

I did a lot of after-school activities in London. I joined the chess club and was pretty good at it. Whenever the school put on any performances, I signed up. My real passion, though, was soccer. I fell in love with soccer and devoted all of my time and attention to it. After school, my classmates and I played soccer for many hours on the school premises. We also practiced for team matches. I was good at scoring goals. I played any forward position but I enjoyed the forward center or right positions the best, because I loved the feeling of giving the ball a really hard kick. When I played forward right, I liked to work my way in at an angle and kick with my right leg. If there weren't any openings for me, I would flick it off to the center so that another player could take a go at it. The game was just super exciting for me.

I didn't know how crazy people were about soccer in London or in the rest of the world until I went to a game and a couple of my friend's older siblings said that we should be careful with our colors...you know, showing them off. If you wore your team's colors, scarves, and wool hats, you ran the risk of kids from opposing teams jumping and attacking you. We had to make sure to enter with fans of the teams we were rooting for. When I went inside the stadium and heard all the loud cheers, it felt like what I imagined the Coliseum in Rome was like during a gladiator spectacle; chaotic, dangerous, energetic, and full of life. Everything about our new life in London was just so cool and exhilarating. My brother and I became so integrated into the culture, we even developed cockney accents!

In London, my mom's infectious personality allowed her to thrive and people really loved her there as well. She made a lot of great friendships in London, including a couple named Pat and Richard. My mom cooked a lot for them and they loved it. My mom had an amazing gift for cooking. Anything she put together had people craving for more, especially when it came to her signature sweet potato pies. Ironically, her own mom had no talent in that area... she couldn't cook at all. They were poor, and when my mom was a little girl, she and her younger brother and sister would look out the window and watch the family next door as they cooked and ate. Sometimes the family would pass them freshly baked bread through the window. My mom was mesmerized by how it looked and smelled, and she never forgot about it. When she was about to get married to her first husband, Donald Hayes, he kept repeating to his family that he wanted to get married near his childhood home in New Jersey. When everyone asked why, he would say, "Because Laurita can't cook and if we get a divorce, it's much easier."

Soon after that, my mom made it her passion to learn how to cook. She bought a Betty Crocker cookbook and made it her personal bible. She also practiced cooking with Donald's sister and mom. She soon became a master of her craft and everyone loved her cooking. Pat and Richard were especially big fans of my mom's cooking, and they introduced her to some English investors who were interested in starting a restaurant. The investors met my mom and fell in love with her. They didn't want her in the kitchen, though; they wanted her to socialize with the patrons.

The investors did everything to get the restaurant going: they found the location, decorated, and also supplied the hardware for cooking and drinks. That was how my mom came to have a soul food restaurant in London called Laurita's. The restaurant opened on Fulham Road in Chelsea in 1971. Chelsea was a very popular location and it was really the hip place to be. Because this new restaurant was the talk of the town, they decided to do 3 opening nights and the press came to all 3. Many celebrities, models, artists, designers and the like were in attendance. Some of the finest actors and performers of the time showed up: Peter O'Toole, Donnie Hathaway, Peter Sellers, Mick Jagger and several of the Rolling Stones, Rod Stewart, Joan and Jackie Collins. They all hung out with my mom and loved going there.

It was a real London celebrity hotspot. There were always big celebrities there like David Bowie, Joan Collins, Mick Jagger, and

Liza Minnelli. Laurita's was the first soul food restaurant in the U.K. and only the second in all of Europe. It was really something new for people at the time...most Europeans had never had this sort of food before. My mom's sweet potato pies became especially legendary. David Hemmings, a famous English actor, promoted her sweet potato pies and helped to give them their legendary status, just because he loved them so much! Unfortunately, however, the business side of things ultimately didn't work out. After a few years, the restaurant closed down. The celebrity crowds, great food, and mama's amazing sweet potato pie weren't enough to keep things going. I'm sure that the myth of that sweet potato pie is still whispered about on the London streets.

While we are on the subject, allow me to digress for a moment to tease you with the taste of my mom's sweet potato pie! It begins with that sweet smell of nutmeg and cinnamon in the oven; it creeps out from the kitchen and into your room, no matter where you may be in the house. It's the calming, deep smell of the sweet potato that makes you feel so warm inside. As my mom sets the pies out on the dinner table, your mouth is drooling with anticipation. But hold on - you have to wait for them to cool down. Patience is a virtue, right? But who has patience and who can resist that orangey brown, sultry, glazy sweet potato pie? As I cut a slice from the tray and watch in awe while the light and flaky crust falls away, I take more than I should. Mmmm...that vanilla smell sneaks up on me as I gently set a piece on my plate. It's love at first sight. I bite into a huge chunk and it slowly melts in my mouth and swirls down my throat and before it hits my stomach, I realize...I need much more of my mama's sweet potato pie! My mom gave me permission to include her recipe for sweet potato pie inside this book. Please try to make it for yourself - I know that you'll enjoy it!

Laurita's Sweet Potato Pie Recipe

<u>Ingredients</u>

3 med sweet potatoes

Dash of salt

half a stick of butter

One egg

Tablespoon of cinnamon

Tsp ground nutmeg

Quarter tsp of allspice

Tsp of ginger

One cup of Organic cane sugar and a cup of organic brown sugar

Two table spoons of vanilla

Can of evaporated milk

If you like coconut, add half a cup

<u>Directions</u>

Boil sweet potatoes till they're very soft, then take off the skin.

Add butter...stir well.

Add spices and sugar.

Then the egg, mix well and then add the can of milk...mix well.

Pour into 9" pie shell and bake at 350.

Get a large mixing bowl and place the sweet potatoes inside oven for anywhere from 60-90 minutes until done.

In some ways, my parents' life in London was very similar to the way that they lived in New York - they were once again immersed in the club world. My parents spent a lot of time at the original London location of the Hard Rock Café, where they befriended the owner, Isaac Tigrett. One night my mom was chatting with friends at the bar while my dad was out in front. My dad turned around because he heard a loud quarrel. My mom was in an argument with a famous English TV host. Apparently, my dad heard people yelling, "He kicked her in the ass!" and he saw people pointing. My dad thought that my mom was being attacked by Isaac Tigrett, so he rushed over and punched Isaac in the face. The whole crowd yelled, "No, it's the other guy!" My dad, wearing a tight satin tuxedo (it was 1971, after all), ended up getting in a wild tussle with this TV host. My dad told me it was very embarrassing because he didn't have underwear on and during the fight, his pants split in the back and exposed his rear end. I guess it was just another day in a Chelsea bar.

My mom had many celebrity friends in London. One of them was David Bowie, because my mom was tight with his wife, Angie Bowie. Angie was full of energy and I remember her being very nice, artistic and fun to be around. I used to play with their son Zowie Bowie, who is now better known as the film director Duncan Jones. My brother and I really liked David Bowie a lot. He had this cool and charismatic charm that just immediately won you over. One day, when my brother was about 10 years old, he ran away from home. No one knew where he could have gone, but I guessed that he must have run away to Bowie's house. I went over to Bowie's place and, sure enough, my brother was there. Bowie was really nice to him and he took the time to talk to him and let him hang out there for a bit. Our parents eventually figured out where we were, and they showed up to pick us up. Bowie was extremely gracious about the whole thing, and it's a little story that my brother will definitely never forget!

At some point during our stay in London, my dad started hanging out with an English bloke of questionable reputation. One day, they were walking through Chelsea and they passed a medieval church, where they saw a large, old, beat up-looking wooden coat-of-arms lying by the side of the church. They thought if they cleaned it up, they could make a good penny. Of course, at the same time, they didn't think to check to see if the church still wanted it. When my dad's English pal took it to a dealer, the dealer had already seen an article about the stolen coat-of-arms in the local Police Gazette. The dealer called the police and they brought the English gentleman to the precinct for questioning. When my dad found out what had happened, he told my mom that he knew this friend would rat him out to save himself. He also knew that the fact that he was an American would make the police be especially harsh on him. My dad told my mom that if the cops came, he would go out the back door and fly back to the U.S. to avoid getting arrested. When the police finally came knocking on our door, that's just what he did. My dad quickly told my mom that he would come back in a few months once things had calmed down.

While my dad was away, my mom began dating a German professional boxer. When my dad came back, he was furious with my mom and they got into huge fight over it. It was a loud brawl and the neighbor called the cops. The neighbors told the police that there was a warrant out on my dad – he was still wanted for the theft of that coat-of-arms, remember - and he was arrested. He spent the next four months in prison. While in prison, he had to pick potatoes on a farm every day. He and the other inmates read about the success of Laurita's Restaurant in the paper, and my dad bragged to everyone, "That's my wife! I got the investors to put the money up!" They all just laughed at and brushed his comments off like he was crazy. It was definitely a serious low point in my dad's life.

When he got out of prison, he and my mom were barely on speaking terms, and she wouldn't let him stay with her. My dad had nowhere to go, so he stayed with Christine Keeler, a family friend. She was a topless showgirl, model and high class prostitute, and she is best known for her involvement with a married government official named John Profumo, the Secretary of State for War in the U.K.

government. This was a scandalous situation, because she was also involved with a Soviet diplomat. It was the height of the Cold War and everyone was afraid that these relationships had led to a security breach. After a shooting incident between two of Keeler's other lovers, she was investigated by the press, which resulted in Profumo giving testimony to the House of Commons. The whole incident was called the Profumo Affair and it led to the discrediting of Harold Macmillan's Conservative government. The story was later made into the British film *Scandal*, starring Joanne Whalley, Bridget Fonda and John Hurt. Keeler was an infamous and legendary figure...my parents really ran with the biggest, wildest, most counterculture people they could. Keeler helped my dad and let him stay with her until he got his head together. My dad was broke and he had no college degree to help him land a good job, so he had to once again fall back on his artistic abilities to make ends meet. He began refinishing tables and sprucing up old antiques.

In the end, there was just too much strain on my parents' marriage, and they decided to separate again. My dad was upset about the break-up, but he was also excited about meeting new women. He would constantly meet girls on the street and immediately bring them home. When my brother and I walked with him down the street – we were roughly 7 or 8 at the time – he would spot a girl and get that romantic, intense look in his eyes. My brother and I knew that look and we knew what he was about to do. We would grab him, saying, "Ah man, c'mon, no, dad! Stop!" We would literally pull the shirt off his chest as he ran towards the lady to meet her. He told us that when we were older, we'd be doing the same thing.

One time, my dad took us to a park. He started talking to a woman, and he told my brother and me that he was "going to go talk to this girl for a little while" and that he'd be right back. Meishan and I looked at each other and thought, "Yeah, talk." Eventually it got late, so we decided to go home. We snuck in, knowing very well what our dad was up to in the bedroom. We came up with a good idea to play a trick on him. We took out a couple of flashlights and burst into the bedroom, where we caught them in the act. My brother and I laughed, saying, "Ahh, you're going to talk, huh?" We knew we were embarrassing him so we ran back into our rooms…he was pissed, as one might imagine.

I remember a scary moment from when my parents were separated: I was walking with my mom and we were with her new boyfriend, the German boxer. My dad was in the area and saw us, and he immediately became angry. My sister Naria was on the boxer's shoulders and my dad didn't like that. One thing led to another, and after my dad and the boxer started arguing, they got into a fistfight. My dad was a tough man and didn't back down, even though his opponent was a skilled fighter. When he felt that the boxer was getting the better of him, he ran into a nearby liquor shop and then came out with a bottle of liquor. He broke the bottle on a lamppost and chased the guy down the street with it. It was a pretty scary event for me to witness - I was only 8 years old.

After a couple more years, when I was about 10, my mom moved to Paris with my sisters, Naria and Taiesha, who were 4 and 2 years-old. My dad decided to go to Rome and he took my brother and me with him. He thought that it would be better for his sons to be around their dad. It was a tough time for both of my parents and it wasn't so easy for me. On my first day in Rome, I got into a fight with a kid who was making fun of my Afro (what can I say, it was the early 70's and I had a big Afro). Afterwards, my dad found him and declared that we would never fight again and that we were going to be friends. That definitely was not going to happen - the other kid and I really didn't like each other - but my dad's intensity and his forceful attitude were so persuasive that he scared both of us and we kept our distance from each other.

Rome was a pretty wild and exciting place, and there was always something happening. My brother and I used to hang out in the Roman piazzas and just take it all in. In Rome's Trastevere neighborhood, there were people and restaurants just about everywhere you looked, and the cultural atmosphere was just amazing. There were these guys we thought were pretty cool and who were nice to us, but we later learned that they were part of a small group of criminals who hung out in the corner of the piazzas in one of the restaurants, eating or having coffee. They weren't just relaxing and hanging out, though; they were always in the middle of planning their next move and scoping out the tourists they thought might be good pick pocket victims.

A lot of tourists frequented this area of Rome because there were monuments, beautiful fountains and other stunning places of interest. Many tourists loved to dress to the nines and carry brand name accessories. They spent a lot of money, and their expensive tastes were a hint to the local gangs that this was someone worth stealing from. The gang members would get on a Vespa, with one guy in the front and one in the back. When a tourist couple walked around the Piazza taking in the sights, the woman would normally have her handbag lazily hanging off her shoulder or on her arm. The two guys on the Vespa would ride by slowly and yank the purse and drive off. The couple would give chase but never had any luck, because they would never be able to catch a scooter on foot. The gang members never got arrested, though – I suspect that they must have had an understanding with the local cops.

This was a daily activity. Sometimes a robbery would happen at noon and again later that night. We would see the same guys sitting at those local cafés or restaurants. It was an event that my brother and I liked to wait around and observe, because it was so exciting and sudden. We were just kids, and we didn't realize how nasty it all really was; one second these people were minding their own business (though, honestly, it's probably not a good idea to show off your wealth in that kind of area!) and the next second they were totally distraught.

Another time, I was on a Vespa myself, riding around and having fun. I realized that there was a robbery in progress and the lady being robbed was running after the robbers on their Vespa. Funny enough, their Vespa conked out as they were trying to get away! The robber in the back jumped off while the driver tried to restart the bike. Before you knew it, the lady who got robbed was able to catch up to the bike and she began smacking the driver in the face and head. The other robber started running towards me - maybe he wanted to hijack my Vespa? I took a quick U-turn and headed out of there! That was a close call...it wasn't funny in the moment, but my friends and I laughed about it afterwards.

My mom and dad tried to make their relationship work again, so she came to Rome to live with us. My mom's ability to meet and make amazing friends was no different in Rome. There was an Italian guy named Valentino, who would dress like the actor Valentino from the silent movie era, and he would always wear ruby red lipstick as an artistic statement. My brother and I liked him, though we were always embarrassed when he would take us to the market to shop, all the while singing an opera piece loudly through the streets. He had a serious operatic voice and was a fan favorite in the neighborhood. I would try to cover my face so my friends didn't see me, but people would hear his voice from inside their houses. They would open their windows, laughing and screaming, "Valentino! Valentino!" Of course, this only egged him on and made him sing even louder.

My parents were friends with a lot of other eccentric, artistic, magnetic people, and there were always huge parties at our apartment. I met the first black woman to be on the cover of Vogue magazine, Donyale Luna. I developed the biggest crush on her, and I was mesmerized by her sultry lips. She used to give me marijuana even though I was only 12. When she passed me the joint, she would always say, "Chika-Boom." I also met the legendary film director, Federico Fellini. He took me on a tour of Cinecitta, the famous Italian studio, and I saw many actors in incredible costumes. Fellini himself was a larger than life guy, and being on those sets was like walking into the most vivid, bold, brightly colored painting of all time.

Around this time, my family visited Naples and we had a strange little episode happen to us there. I was innocently walking through the streets with my siblings when suddenly, for no apparent reason, people started to follow us around. They stared at us like we were the biggest celebrities in the world. I had no idea what they must have been thinking! We kept walking through the city and the crowd around us slowly got bigger and bigger. Before long, we had a huge audience – they were following us everywhere we went, pointing at us, shouting, and taking pictures. It was interesting and funny at the same time. For some reason, I didn't feel threatened by it at all. It was like we were in a dream or in a movie!

These years in Europe gave me a true appreciation for diversity and for embracing life. There's always something unique about every country in the world, and I learned how to step outside of my own perspective to see things in a new way. The English had a unique celebratory kind of way about them, a sense of glory and patriotism. They were so proud of their traditions, Shakespeare, and all the glory of the British monarchy. When it came to Italy, I couldn't begin to find the words to describe all of the beauty and culture and great food. I wish I could properly tell you about the warmth you feel everywhere and about the creativity that was embedded in the tiles of the ancient buildings and romantic cobblestone streets. You see the history of the Roman Empire everywhere around you. It was just a magical place to be.

I was inspired by all this creativity and these colorful experiences, but life at home wasn't always easy. I was constantly fighting with my brother, and just being around him was a challenge that filled me with fear and nervousness. It may not seem unusual for brothers to fight, but these fights were more brutal than you might imagine. They were definitely a critical source of the stress and anxiety that

I felt as a kid. Let me give you an example of a typical day coming home from school. After I got out of school, there were a couple of hours where no one was home except for my brother and me. Each and every day, I knew that I would be coming home to some kind of conflict over something. For example, Meishan and I would argue over whose turn it was to do chores, whether it was doing the laundry, cleaning our room, or any number of things. I'd walk in the door and my brother would say, "Why didn't you do the laundry or dishes?" and I would remind him that he was supposed to do it. Next thing you knew, we were on the floor, wrestling and fighting. He was two years-older than I was and would usually get the better of me.

Whenever my dad came home and found us fighting, he would grab us by the necks, pull us apart, and angrily shout, "You guys want to fight?!" Then he'd take us to a more spacious area in the apartment and say, "Okay, fight!" as if it was of prizefight or something. We would fight again, and when I was losing my dad would stop us and then lecture us about fighting. It never made sense to me. My dad really didn't understand the emotional impact of all this on a 9 year-old boy. I was very shy as a kid, probably as a result of all of this fighting, bullying, and the beatings.

I didn't know it, but I was looking for a hero and I was looking for strength. The constant bullying weighed really heavily on me. Unfortunately, I became more depressed when my parents finally broke up for the last time. My mom decided that it was time for her to move on, and their relationship finally ended after fourteen years together. My mom started dating another man and everything just fell apart. Dad went back to New York and he didn't speak to my mom for many years. My siblings and I were just kids, but we had become used to it. The constant break-ups and arguments had become normal for us. Still, we could tell that this time it was really over for good, and it hit us hard. It was all so confusing and demoralizing. I felt like I couldn't breathe. I had lost faith.

The months went by and my parents eventually decided that my brother and I should go live with our dad in New York. It had been an emotional time for us, and we very much wanted to see our dad again – it had already been around six months or so since we had been together. We headed back to New York and our European adventure was over for now. I felt confused and dejected and I needed something that would pick my spirits up. I had to become stronger and I needed to challenge myself. I would soon have the chance to achieve that sense of inner strength by jumping into something that became an absolutely essential part of my life: the practice of martial arts.

Pop

So close my memories of past full and bright

So close my memories I was never uptight

When Pop was there, there was no wrong just right

"You're *The Greatest* my son, there is no doubt"

With you in my corner I won every bout

But as I grew older I had to see that it was with me to learn life

And only with me

Your struggles to show me just led me astray

To say "Pop, I'm a man, I'll lead my way"

So here I am a warrior and strong

Dipping and dashing and sliding along

Knowing one day I'll be a pop just like you, having

kids of my own

Can't wait for them to see you

But before that day comes your seed still remains so

powerful it is

I must make my claim

The Greatest I'll become and not just for me

For Pop, my lord, just wait and see

Chapter 3 - Coming Home

*"I believe in everything until it's disproved. So I
believe in fairies, the myths, dragons. It all exists,
even if it's in your mind. Who's to say that dreams
and nightmares aren't as real as the here and now?"*

John Lennon

My brother and I arrived back in New York in 1976, and we met our
dad in Far Rockaway, on the border of Coney Island. We were really
happy to see him again, but it was a bittersweet moment. We were
in a rough part of town, and we walked right into the middle of a
violent crime. I suddenly saw a gang of guys chase after a single
guy. The chased man ran right past me. I never forgot it, because
that was the first time I saw, close-up, what it looks like when a man
has real fear in his eyes. In a flash, everything was silent. The other
gangsters all pounced on that solitary, lonely guy and, it appeared
to me, stabbed him. I desperately wanted to help him out, but I was
just a kid. It wasn't so much that I felt scared for our lives or that I
was worried about what might happen to us. What struck me was the
primal, intense desperation of the situation and how hopeless I felt.
It was a terrifying and shocking thing to experience.

That instance of violence, even though it happened so many years ago, made a huge impact on me and is still a powerful memory. I didn't realize it at the time, but it was definitely a traumatic moment. As I grew older and I started to observe why my guard was up in so many situations and why I was often so defensive when there was no need to be, I was able to trace many of my feelings back to that sudden flash of brutality. It was a moment where I recognized a need to defend myself and to learn how to protect myself and other people. In a way, it marked the end of my childhood.

It was around this time - as I experienced my brother's bullying and all of these scenes of violence - that I became really interested in superheroes and action stars. I remember going to school and running home to read comics because I was mesmerized by superheroes like Superman, Batman, and Spider-Man, and I loved the Hercules movies. I was so fascinated by the whole thing! I used to read superhero comics a lot, and I particularly remember this ad that was featured in a lot of issues. There was a scrawny guy on the beach with his girlfriend. They are lying together on a blanket when a strong looking, muscular bully comes over and kicks sand in the scrawny guy's face and takes his girl. The scrawny guy, obviously upset, starts lifting weights and gets himself strong. He goes back to the beach to teach the guy a lesson and get his girl back. I was fascinated by these strong stories of ordinary people lifting themselves up to become their own hero.

As time went on and I settled back into the New York life, I got a certain amount of stability. My dad had a new girlfriend named Jackie, who I really liked, and who had a young daughter named

Running the NYC Marathon

Sybelle. Jackie and my dad would actually later have a baby together: a little girl named Nefertiti. It started to feel like a little family after a while, and our household seemed steadier than what I was used to. It was a good feeling. At the same time, my dad let my brother and I run wild on the streets of New York. We had a lot of independence to explore and try things out, even though crime was high and things could get dangerous.

I really had to adjust when I got to my first day of school. I mean, it was a culture shock all over again. The kids were tough and mean, and I had gotten used to the quieter and mellower European attitude. I had a cockney accent and wore tight blue corduroy bell-bottom jeans with white stars on them. I was always getting into fights because of kids picking on me. There was no soccer...just basketball and the playgrounds, so I had to find other things to do.

My brother and I lead separate lives when we got back to New York, even though we both went to the same junior high school and high school. He had his friends and I had mine...at the same time, of course, we still shared a certain amount of family loyalty. There was one incident where my brother unexpectedly proved that loyalty to me. When I was 14, there was a class bully named Lloyd; most kids were his friends out of fear and others, like me, just stayed away from him. He had a maturity that was beyond his years. He was more like a 25 year-old. It wasn't that he was super tall...his body was a little stronger and he was mentally very different from most of the other kids.

We had Spanish class with a teacher who was a happy-go-lucky Latino guy who gave us a lot of leeway and we would all have fun with him. It was a really nice class. During one class, Lloyd began making fun of me; I can't recall the specific interaction, but I remember it was something about my answer to the teacher's question. I looked at him and told him to shut up. I knew that I couldn't physically take him, but I wanted to look good in front of Yvette Nieves, a girl who I had a crush on. Lloyd told me to step outside and so I did. I was ready to go, but he jumped on me right away and punched me right in the eye. The Spanish teacher was a pretty big guy and he grabbed us both at the same time and pulled us apart with ease. Lloyd never bothered me again, so I assumed that our little beef was over. But then I found out that it was because of my brother. My brother found out what happened, and when he saw Lloyd in the lunch room, he literally kicked Lloyd's ass and even continued to kick him even when he fell down and couldn't fight back. My brother was pretty wild when he was angry. I was surprised he stood up for me though, since we didn't get along. It made me feel good.

At 16, I became the captain of the fencing team in Brandeis High School. It wasn't that I was the greatest fencer: it was just that it was a small class of only 6 or 7 students, and I was better than everyone else in the class. I really enjoyed fencing and it gave me an early understanding of how to implement linear timing movements into the martial arts techniques that I would use later on in my life. I also learned how to figure out how to choose the proper angles of attack by using a fencing tool called the foil. I also really liked putting on the fencing outfit, and the whole thing was a positive experience for me.

I had a tall friend on the team that liked to pretend that we were in a swashbuckling, Shakespearean-type old adventure movie. We would fence with each other, fighting up and down the school hallways that were empty after school hours. We would make up our own dialogue and shout lines like, "Meet me on the bridge!" or "How dare hath thoughest fightest with me! I'm the mostest strongest in this here village!" Then we would charge at each other and fight it out. We had a ball.

My family lived in a hotel on 45th Street, just off of Sixth Avenue, called the St. James Hotel. It wasn't particularly nice but it was pretty clean. There were two rooms, a bedroom and a living room. The living room was pretty big and that's where me, my brother, and Jackie's daughter Sybelle all slept. My dad and Jackie took the bedroom. If you looked out the living room window, you could see over all of 45th Street. It was right off the center of Times Square and would get pretty busy on Friday and Saturday nights.

Living in that area was an education for a teenaged kid. Jackie and my dad used to set up a stand and table to sell trinkets and things on the street in Times Square. My dad was making ends meet by selling his gold lamé handbags that he designed himself. They were pretty popular. The famous Italian designer Fiorucci actually got a hold of one of them and started producing them. There was a brothel down the block from the St. James Hotel (there were brothels all over the place in Times Square during those days, especially because of all of the porn movie theaters in the area) and my dad used to sell his handbags to the women in the brothel.

I went to all of these places with my dad and acted as his sales assistant. My brother was a cerebral type of kid and didn't find his passion until much later than me, so he acted lazy and disinterested, and gave our dad a hard time because he didn't want go out and work. My dad complained about it but didn't push it, so it was my responsibility to pick up the slack and help our dad out. When we went to the brothels, I wouldn't really see anything unsavory. There was always an area upstairs with a room and a desk where women would sit down and no sex was going on. That would happen in other rooms, further back somewhere.

One time one of the girls asked if I would go buy her a hot dog. I said sure and when I came back she gave me a tip. I liked the idea of being able to make some extra money for myself, so now and then I would go back up there and do a few errands for her and some of the other girls. They were all really nice, regular girls, even though I knew that their job was supposed to be looked down on. We got along great!

I watched a lot of martial arts movies during those teenage years and Bruce Lee was my absolute inspiration (Bruce's Chinese name, by the way, is Xiaolong, which means Little Dragon). The excitement I got from watching him move on the screen was more than inspiring - it was life-changing. I joined an after-school program called The Door, and I started to learn Aikido there under the tutelage of a martial artist named Ralph King. I learned wristlocks and throws, and it was completely fascinating to me. However, the style wasn't quite the same as what I saw Bruce Lee do in his films. I wanted to move like him; I wanted to kick like him; I wanted to jump through the air like him! He was a living, breathing superhero, and he was everything that I wanted to be. There were a lot of actors that I liked at the time: Steve McQueen, Paul Newman, Marlon Brando, Sammy Davis Jr., Robert Redford, Sidney Poitier, Steve Reeves, and others were huge for me, and they helped me to light an inner fire of creativity and expression. But Bruce Lee was on another level – in his case, the fire was more like an explosion.

During this time, I heard that, if you wanted learn a martial arts style that was filled with high-flying kicks, you should get into the Korean style of Tae Kwon Do. I found a Tae Kwon Do school on the Upper East Side of Manhattan called Richie Chun's. My dad gave me the money to join, and I got a new uniform and a new belt. I was in heaven! I trained there for over a year and a half and reached the level of brown belt. Eventually, I began competing in tournaments and winning trophies! I got disqualified during some of these tournaments for kicking back too hard. We were only kids, so they didn't want us getting seriously hurt. I didn't realize what I was doing because I didn't know my own strength. On a certain level, I was also lashing out after years of abuse and bullying, and I was expressing a lot of pent-up physicality. I also became a boxing gym rat, working out at my stepdad's boxing club in Times Square. All of this exercise was in addition to me joining the fencing and wrestling teams at school. The idea of training and exercising had become a true outlet for me to get away from the stresses of my young life.

The difficulties that I had experienced at a young age – my parent's rollercoaster marriage, the abuse from Aunt Ethel, my mom's excessive disciplinary measures, my brother's bullying – drove me on and on to train harder and get better. My childhood definitely had a huge impact on the reason why I began training. I didn't realize just how much of an impact it really was until I was a lot older and I began to deal with my insecurity and self-esteem issues. The abuse I suffered made me feel weak inside and I wanted to feel strong. I had a psychological and emotional need to learn how to protect myself. I wanted to be strong like all of the superheroes who I admired so much and martial arts and exercise gave me the chance to grow stronger.

If I was passionate about my martial arts training, I was just as passionate about martial arts movies. I would leave school and go straight to 42nd Street on Times Square. Today, Times Square is a glossy, Disney-like tourist destination. At that time, though, it was considered to be the asshole of the earth. There were porn films in almost every movie theater on the strip between 7th and 8th Avenues and there were drug dealers and prostitutes everywhere. When you went inside a movie theater, it was dark and creepy, with sticky floors and cheap plastic seats. It was gross, but they played every kung fu film being produced at the time, especially stuff by the legendary Shaw Brothers studio. It was just amazing. I loved *8 Diagram Pole Fighter*, *Five Deadly Venoms*, *Shaolin Master Killer*, *The Street Fighter*, and many others. The films were all shown on grainy, scratchy 35mm reels, and they had this grimy look to them that I'll never forget. The movies had brilliant choreography; sometimes great directing; and occasionally a memorable story, but usually not. They mostly just had great martial arts moves. That's what it was all about!

Here is some history on the Shaw Brothers studio. I saved you from having to look it up, because their movies were too important to me to leave anything to chance! The studio was created by the four Shaw brothers from Hong Kong – Runme, Runde, Runje, and Run Run – and they pioneered the art of quickly-made, effective, exciting filmmaking. They had the foresight to recognize that films were going to eventually be a huge business, and they started producing and distributing movies across Southeast Asia all the way back in 1925 by forming the Shaw Corporation. The brothers became more and more successful throughout the years, and by the mid-1960's, they had the money to build a massive movie studio in Hong Kong's Clear Water Bay. The huge studio campus was called Movietown and for some time it was the largest privately-owned movie studio in the world. Movietown was filled with dozens of permanent sets that the studio could use in their historical epics and martial arts action thrillers.

Many famous and influential directors got their start at Shaw Brothers. For instance, director Chang Cheh was known for his bloody, hyper-masculine kung fu movies like *The One-Armed Swordsman* and *Crippled Avengers*. He liked to work with a group of guys that are popularly known as the Venom Mob because they were all in his film *Five Deadly Venoms*. Chang Cheh's protégé was the legendary action director John Woo, who would go on to make classic action movies like *Hard Boiled* and *The Killer* starring Chow

Yun-Fat. In these films, Woo incorporated his master's signature themes of crime, mystery, and stories of righteous men who get caught up in violent situations. One of my favorite directors from the studio was Lau Kar-leung, who discovered a great star named Chia-Hui Liu (also known as Gordon Liu). Gordon Liu was famous for playing heroic Shaolin monks who fought against the injustice of cruel governments. Quentin Tarantino paid homage to Gordon Liu by casting him in the *Kill Bill* films as Pai Mei, the martial arts master who trains Uma Thurman.

Some people didn't like the Shaw Brothers movies because of the usually recycled and predictable plots or because the dubbing into the English language was so horrid. However, I was only 14 when I first saw a Shaw Brothers movie and it really helped to inspire me to train as a kid. It also made the whole concept of training really fun, because I'd imagine that I was one of the stars of their films at the Shaolin Temple somewhere training alongside some of the great kung fu heroes. It's still a dream of mine to work with Asian stars like Stephen Chow (*Kung Fu Hustle*, *Shaolin Soccer*) and Donnie Yen (*Ip Man* films, *Hero*), because I admire their work.

Alright, history lesson over - back to my life. The culture in these Times Square movie theaters was hilarious. People would come from almost everywhere to entertain themselves in the movie theater. I mean you could pay $2 or $3 and watch two or three movies! People would shout out loud, talk about the story, and make crazy comments. There was always some loud and funny guy commenting on the martial arts moves in the films. These guys would shout out stuff like, "I bet he's going to bust out the snake move to whoop his ass!" or, "Smack that punk up with your tiger claw!"

I learned a lot of things from these martial arts movies: integrity, courage, work ethic, and the value of peace. The only thing that was missing was that I wanted to see a martial arts movie starring people of color – people who looked like me. As a person of color, it was easy to feel left out when looking for martial arts stars that were black. The first black martial artist that I ever saw in these movies was Jim Kelly in Bruce Lee's *Enter the Dragon* (his other credits include *Black Belt Jones* and *Three the Hard Way*), and I've been a fan ever since. He had a famous line in *Enter the Dragon* that I really loved: "I don't waste my time with it. When it comes, I won't even notice. I'll be too busy looking good." He made many movies and was the first black action star to sign a deal with Warner Bros.

I had always wanted to meet Jim, and I finally got the chance many years later and it was a great experience that I'll always treasure. Jim was a private person and he didn't frequent Hollywood parties and those sorts of things, so I never got a chance to meet him. However, in 2013, I did an autograph signing at a comic book convention and Jim was there too. A friend of mine arranged to have Jim and I sit at tables that were directly next to each other. We took some pictures together and he said to me, "I always wanted to meet you too, Taimak." It was an amazing thing to hear. He and I talked about martial arts techniques and we had fun watching a few tournament fights that I had on video. It was really cool. We planned to meet again, but I found out from a friend of mine that Jim wanted me to know that he was ill and didn't have long to go. Unfortunately, he passed later that year.

My other major black hero during those early years was Muhammad Ali. He stretched the consciousness of what it meant to be a black person in America during a very challenging time. Ali never spoke with any hate or bitterness about his experiences as a black man, even though he was a realist and knew there was hate in the world. Instead, he spoke with authority, responsibility and grace; he was a goofball at heart, but he still carried himself with total respect and class. He was simply an admirable role model in every way. As kids, we would all gather around the television to watch his fights. We loved to see him move with such ease and grace like a ballet dancer. We loved it even more when he made us laugh by partnering with sports journalist and former attorney Howard Cosell.

I'll never forget watching Ali's classic fight with George Foreman, a bout that was dubbed the Rumble in the Jungle. It was an amazing time in sports history and it was a huge moment for me as a kid. The dictator of what was at that time the Republic of Zaire had agreed to host the fight, and he was going to pay $5 million each to the fighters. I watched every moment on television, eating up all of the hype for it. I loved watching Ali parading across Zaire, with all his African fans chanting the memorable phrase, "Ali, bomaye!" which meant "Ali, kill him!" in Lingala. I was 10 years-old when I saw Ali win that fight. I was absolutely ecstatic and it's one of my greatest childhood memories.

When I competed in my Tae Kwon Do matches, I felt just like Bruce Lee or Muhammad Ali, even though I got disqualified every once in a while for kicking or punching too hard. I was young, but I was heavy handed and didn't know it. I thought that I could just hit as hard as I wanted! I was thrashing and exploding and acting out and just fighting for my life in every tournament. I was like a ball of free energy and I still had to attain a certain amount of discipline. I needed to be mentored and I needed some guidance so that I could control my strength and grow into a more balanced fighter and person.

While I was training and learning more about martial arts, I became fascinated by a karate champion who was also a kung fu movie star named Ron Van Clief. Ron had starred in a martial arts movie called *The Black Dragon* (and was thus also nicknamed Black Dragon), and I wanted to meet him. Aside from Jim Kelly, I had never seen another black man on screen doing martial arts. Ron, just like Jim, looked like a real fighter, and I was so impressed with him. I told my dad about Ron and I was shocked when my dad said he actually knew him! My dad knew a lot of people in New York back then, through selling luxury clothes and art…he even designed stage outfits for The Sugar Hill Gang, a legendary rap group. These jobs allowed him to meet plenty of interesting folks. As a kid, one thing I loved about my dad was that, whatever I was excited about, he made sure he did his best to get it for me. So my dad said, "Yeah, I'll introduce you to Ron" and he immediately went out and made it happen.

My dad and I went to Ron's dojo in the lower eastside of Manhattan. I was expecting some huge loft with a big sign that said *KARATE: Ron Van Clief*, *World Champion* and *Kung Fu Film Star*. It was actually a basement, tucked away completely out of sight, with no advertising at all. We had to really search to find it! When we went in, though, it was an amazing experience. Ron was immediately friendly, and my dad told him that I was interested in martial arts and would love to train with him. He looked at me, smiled, and said, "Great!" He put some gloves on me and I started hitting things. I hit everything I could get my feet or hands on! It was like I was instantly at peace, like I had found the calling that I had been searching for. Ron was a supportive mentor and teacher, and I kept training with him, on and off, for the next 20 years.

Even though I was just a teenager, I put my martial arts training into practice by working as a bouncer. I have a lot of stories from those days, and some of my funniest memories are about a fellow bouncer named Doc Williams. He was a wild, unique, larger-than-life person - exactly the sort of cat that inspired Louis Venosta to create Sho'nuff in *The Last Dragon*! Doc had also trained with Ron, and he was a notorious bully who liked to throw his weight around. He was a big guy, about 6'4" and around 250 lbs., so he could pretty much do whatever he wanted and bully people as he saw fit. I say he was a bully because it wasn't just that he didn't back down from any type of confrontation...he actually instigated them. People were scared of him, and he liked that! Doc and I wound up working together as bouncers at the same club. When he was at the door of the club and he saw someone too close to the rope, he would physically push them and say, "Move back" in his deep and intimidating voice. If they didn't comply, they were in for a possible face bashing.

One time I got to work a little earlier than normal and he was there. He said, "Hey Taimak, come to the back. I want to show you something." He took me to the back and I had no idea what he was going to show me. He rarely dealt with me and I didn't even know that he knew my name! He pulled out his back pack and began to open it up. I was wondering if he had a pet rat in there or something, but when I looked inside I saw what looked like a train track. Doc had a mischievous smile on his face as he slowly pulled this train track out of his bag, and then he pulled out another train track that was attached to the first one by a chain. He had welded these two train tracks together to make nunchucks out of them! He looked at me smiling and twirling them around like he was Bruce Lee or something. As I looked at him, I said to myself, "I better stay way clear of this maniac."

A few months after that, I was preparing to compete at a karate tournament. I was in the bleachers with my friend because I didn't have to fight for another hour or so, and we were just hanging out. That's when I looked down at the crowd and saw Doc walking around in a full gi and a gang of four cronies. He didn't come to compete...he just wanted to start trouble! As he walked around, he looked up and it looked like he was looking at me. I tried to avoid his stare, but my friend said, "Yo Taimak, he's lookin' at you." I said, "Yeah, I know." Doc extended his arm up and pointed his finger directly at me, then curled it back as if to say, come here. I thought to myself, "Oh brother, what does this fool want, why did he pick me?" Doc wasn't actually a fool. On the contrary, he was a very intelligent cat - he just liked to fight. I wasn't going to back down so I walked down the bleachers to see what he wanted. I came up to him and he said, "Follow me." I thought, "Wherever he's taking me, it doesn't seem like it's going to be fun".

He took me to the side of the bleachers and then he did a full big bow and then went into his fighting stance. He shouted in his ominous, Darth Vader-sounding voice, "Defend yourself!" and started attacking me. Even though I was caught off guard and I was scared of his power, I was much faster than him and I easily eluded all of his strikes. Doc got angry and tried to kick my head off. That's when I stopped and said, "Hey Doc, what's going on?" and he said angrily, "You've got a big ego." I didn't know what to say, so I just told him that I didn't want to continue down this path with him. He stared at me for a minute and then walked away. I thought to myself, "Thank God I survived that one."

I remember there was a time when Doc came to my rescue, though. I made it to the finals of a martial arts tournament. I was going to fight the U.S. champion, and there was a $1,000 prize purse for the winner! I was beating him and I needed one more point. This wasn't a full contact match; you could hit your opponent's body as hard as you wanted and you could kick to the head, but if you punched the face with malicious intent or drew blood you would get disqualified. I scored the last point and I was super excited! I beat the U.S. Champion and I was going to get all that prize money! But then, the champion didn't allow the judges to give me that point. He took out his mouthpiece and showed the judges that there was blood on it. There was only a very little bit of blood. In fact, there was really barely anything at all! It was a cowardly way to get out of losing the fight and taking the prize purse. All of a sudden, I heard a big voice say, "THAT'S BULLSHIT!" It was Doc Williams! He came down from the stands and started cursing the judges out. I was shocked, but I was happy that someone was in my corner, especially because Doc's larger-than-life presence made a lot of these guys nervous. It didn't matter though. My opponent had been on the martial arts circuit for many years and he knew the judges well. I was disqualified, but I gained the friendship of Doc Williams. He was such a crazy dude, though, that I wasn't sure whether or not it was a good thing!

One time, Doc told me to meet him on the deuce (that's what folks in the know called 42nd Street). He wanted to see a kung fu movie in one of those dive theaters that I loved so much. We went into a Shaw Brothers flick, and I soon saw a martial artist who I knew from one of the gyms. He said, "Hey Taimak, what's up, bro! It's so dark that I didn't even know it was you." I said hello, but tried to keep a bit of distance – you never knew what would happen when Doc was around.

My friend was talkative, though, and he began talking to me about training in Brooklyn. Doc decided to join in on the discussion. He cut my poor pal off and said (with a demeanor that combined Darth Vader and Dracula), "So you're a martial artist huh?" The guy said yes, and Doc said, "Oh" in a condescending tone. My friend took offence and snickered a bit. I tried to cut in, because I knew there would be trouble, but Doc put his hand on my chest as if to say, stay out of this. I knew something was about to go down and I did my best to stop it, but my friend wasn't going to back down, even though he probably knew he should. My pal repeated, with a bit of bravado, "Yeah, I'm a martial artist." Doc said, "How would you like to come out of the theater and show me your style?"

I tried to hold Doc back, but he didn't respond. Doc got up and told the guy to come with him and we all walked out into the lobby and then downstairs to the bathroom area where there was a lot of room. At that point, Doc looked at the guy and said, "HOLD YOUR STANCE!" My friend got nervous and said, "Listen, I don't want any problems." Doc wasn't going to let him go, though. He shouted, "It's too late, you got a problem now" and then hit the dude with an uppercut that sent him flying back about 8 feet. The poor guy landed right on his ass! Doc yelled at him, "YOU'RE LUCKY YOU AIN'T ANY LIGHTER SKINNED THAN ME OR IT WOULD'VE BEEN MUCH WORSE!"

I met a bunch of other wild and interesting characters during my early years in martial arts. I hung out at so many different gyms, and people came in from all levels of society and from every different background. In addition to my time with Ron Van Clief and at my stepdad's boxing club, I also started going to City Star Kickboxing in Queens. Even though it was about 45 minutes away by train and was always freezing in the gym, it was one of the only reputable kickboxing spots with a good trainer. Yoel Judah, a three-time kickboxing champion and the father of former top boxer Zab Judah, would come to spar with me and other members of the gym. It was run by a short Latin guy named Eddie Encarnacion who never smiled and I was told that he used to be in the revolutionary army in El Salvador.

I was exploring my feelings and expressing myself with all of this martial arts training, the fire burning inside of me. I had really found peace as I trained. It gave me confidence and put me in the right direction. My life was starting to gain momentum, and I was feeling good about how things were going. But I was still a kid, and I had a long way to go.

One of the biggest setbacks of my youth, though, was the day I found out that Bruce Lee had died, back in 1973. I was crushed. I had a dream of meeting him one day, and now that would never happen. It was like the fire inside me flickered for a bit and almost went out. It was a lonely feeling. But I knew that this wasn't going to stop me. If I couldn't meet Bruce Lee, I could still do my best to be like him and follow in his footsteps!

A Scene from *I've Seen Things*

INT. POLICE ACADEMY - GYM - DAY 3

Detective Ray Larson is teaching a self-defense class to cops. There are 5-10 students taking the class, mostly regulars. Everyone is wearing sweats.

> RAY
> Today we're going to be working on
> Self-Defense Technique #4, defense
> against a knife attack. We worked on
> rhythm last week, everyone's rhythm
> is different, as you saw.

The students' chuckle, some in embarrassment. Ray continues.

> RAY (con't)
> You learned your own rhythm, what
> makes you be on rhythm and what
> doesn't. Self-defense isn't the same
> as a prize fight. Prize fighters have an
> hour or more to prepare themselves
> for a bout. You don't have that luxury,
> you can be attacked from any place, at
> any time, in a split second. You don't
> have time to warm-up. You have to be
> prepared, like an animal in the jungle.

CAMERA PANS ACROSS THE STUDENTS' FACES.

RAY (con't)

OK, let's go over Self-Defense #4.

The students get up and begin. Ray walks around observing and helping the students. He stops next to a pair of them going through the technique.

RAY (con't)
Hold on John, that's not exactly right.
Let me show you.

Ray gestures for JOHN's partner, STEVE, to attack him.

RAY (con't)

Go ahead, Steve.

Ray stands in front of him. Steve attacks Ray with a prop knife, thrusting it toward his belly. Ray pivots and secures Steve's arm under his own, which creates a lever at Steve's elbow. The knife drops out of Steve's hand.

With amazing precision and control, Ray elbows upward to Steve's jaw, coming inches away from his face, and then smoothly turns him down to the ground with a leg sweep. Ray takes his cuffs out and demonstrates the controlling posture.

INT. POLICE ACADEMY - LOCKER ROOM - DAY 4

Ray is changing into his suit. Another cop, OFFICER JOSE PUENTEZ, Latino, 28-35, is getting dressed as well. It's a casual atmosphere in the locker room. The guys are chatting and changing.

JOSE

I get the rhythm thing Ray, but
wouldn't it be a little more fun to go
Salsa? Whatta you think, buddy?

John is standing alongside them smiling, as Jose simulates salsa dancing.

RAY (smiling)

Yeah, I can imagine the guys picking
up some good moves there. Only one
thing is, they'll be picking up a lot
more then that...if you know what I
mean.

JOSE

Yeah. Tequila and women.

The guys in the locker room laugh along with Ray and Jose. They head out.

Chapter 4 - Learning on the Streets

"The medicine for my suffering I had within me from the very beginning but I did not take it. My ailment came from within myself but I did not observe it. Until this moment. Now I see I will never find the light unless, like the candle, I am my own fuel."

Bruce Lee

When you run a race, it's not just about getting from point A to point B. Along the way, you're going to have to overcome a lot of minor obstacles, and you'll experience all sorts of little moments of self-discovery and self-understanding. It's the same thing when it comes to fighting; the training is just as important as the victory. When you push yourself, you naturally learn more about yourself and what you're capable of. My teenage years were filled with these obstacles and moments, and they helped me to grow as a person. It wasn't an easy time and my problems weren't going to be solved in a day...I was starting down a tough road to self-understanding that I wouldn't really comprehend for another twenty years.

When I was 15, I lived in an area that was typical of the Upper West Side of Manhattan. Manhattan is such a densely populated place, which means that very different people and very different lifestyles are placed right next to each other. This area was full of young drug dealers, and sometimes things would get very dangerous. I remember a time when Chuck-O, one of the guys on the block, had a run-in with some drug dealers. Not too long after that, his apartment was sprayed with bullets, narrowly missing his mom. There was definitely a dark side to all of the fun we were having.

Despite the high levels of crime, the area was a popular hang-out for kids from other neighborhoods. While some kids were definitely interested in the drugs, most people liked being part of the social scene there. We had dancing, music, football in the streets, and community trips to places like the Six Flags Great Adventure amusement park in New Jersey. During Halloween, we had vans that would take all of the neighborhood kids to the big Haunted Mansion on the Long Branch boardwalk. We didn't really know how to recognize the social problems and dangers that were around us...we turned a blind eye because we didn't know any better, and we just threw ourselves into the fun, carefree, emotional side of what we were seeing. One of the problems was that there were just a lot of young kids with too much money on their hands; drugs gave them access to a lifestyle that would otherwise have been way out of their reach.

Because of the popularity of Bruce Lee, there were kids on the block that would act as if they knew martial arts. However, the only kids that truly practiced martial arts were a Dominican kid named VG and me. We would go back and forth sparring in the hallways of our buildings, while other kids looked on enjoying our spectacle. VG was about two years-older than I was and he would always have a slight edge over me in our sparring matches. However, I was really competitive with him and it was fun. He was shorter than me and very athletic. He would do pretty outrageous things and to save face in front of the other kids, I would follow up and do the same.

One afternoon, I was hanging out with VG and a few other guys, when VG looked up to the window of an apartment building and pointed at a window that was around 15 feet above street level. VG smirked and said to everybody, "I can jump out of that." I responded, "Are you sure?" He said, "Yeah, watch." All I could think to myself was, "Damn, why do you have to do this?" because I knew I was going to have to do it afterwards! I knew I couldn't back down from his challenge. I had to do it, no matter how scared I was, or else all of the other kids were going to make fun of me. VG went up to the apartment, sat on the ledge, and jumped. His landing was amazing - like a cat. So now it was my turn. I got up to the window, sat on the ledge and said to myself, "Hell, Taimak, you're nuts!" But before I could change my mind, I leapt off the ledge and landed. Not as softly as VG, mind you, but I landed pretty damn well! But I did say to myself then, "I'm not doing THAT one again."

I was always trying to prove myself to the kids around me and I wanted to look like I was a tough, cool guy. I had a lot of shyness that I had to get over, and my self-esteem issues kept me from being confident and self-assured. This was especially true when it came to women. When I wanted to talk to a girl, I almost felt paralyzed, and I didn't have the confidence to believe that any of them would really like me. My first serious crush was on an 18 year-old Latin girl named Carmen Lopez. Carmen was from Queens, but she stayed in our neighborhood over the summer, living with her sister Lisa.

Man, I thought about Carmen all the time! I was only 15 at the time, and I never thought she would go for me.

My friends and I were part of a younger group of guys in the neighborhood, and we used to hang out on a stoop across from Lisa's place. One day, Carmen came out to the street to hang out with her sister and their girlfriends. They were immediately swarmed by a group of guys, while we just stared from across the street. We were out of school for the summer and it was really hot out. My friend nudged me as I looked on and said, "Hey, Taimak. She's looking at you!" I asked who he was talking about, and he pointed at Carmen, "Her, stupid." I couldn't believe it, but it seemed to be true - even though there were all these older guys around her, Carmen's eyes were glued on me. My heart began to beat fast. "This can't be possible," I thought to myself. I was only 15, and there was no way. But it was true! She looked right at me! My buddy saw it too, so I wasn't just imagining things...right?

That weekend, a bunch of us from the neighborhood packed into vans and headed for the Haunted Mansion. I knew Carmen was going too and nothing would stop me from getting close to her. I knew there was another guy who was interested in her - he was 20 - but I wasn't going to let that stop me. I wasn't going to lose focus. When we all got to the haunted house, I found my way to her and we began to walk through the scary hallways. It was very dark, but I got close to Carmen and she got close to me. All the guys were laughing and the girls were screaming. Carmen grabbed me and held me tightly. I loved it! I went from a 15 year-old kid to feeling like a 21 year-old in just one squeeze. When we finally got out of the building, for some

The ledge as it looks today, that VG and I jumped off of.
Never again!

strange reason, I quickly let her go; it was as if I was going to be caught stealing money from a bank.

Why was I so insecure? Sure, I was a couple of years younger than she was, but she was clearly into me. Carmen and I had an unspoken agreement and we made sure we were in the same van on the ride home. We also made sure we were sitting next to each other in the back with all the pillows scattered around. It was dark back there and we put two pillows on top of our laps as we held hands underneath the pillows and snuggled next to each other. I didn't want anybody to see what was going on. Was I embarrassed? Did I feel like a fraud? Did I secretly think that all of these happy feelings would collapse at any second?

We got back to New York at about 5:00 in the morning. Once we reached our block, everyone scattered, returning home after a long night at the Haunted Mansion. I told Carmen I would come back to see her in a few minutes, after everyone left. The street was deserted and the morning light was just starting to peek through the night sky. I waited for a while, making sure that no one else was around. When the coast was clear, I went across the street to Carmen's building. I could see Carmen in the window upstairs, looking down at me. She buzzed me in and we met in the hallway. My heart was pounding as we looked into each other's eyes and then we gently but passionately kissed. It seemed like we were kissing forever! I got her number and went back home to go to sleep.

The next day, I told my friend what happened. He couldn't believe it, but he loved the story and was overjoyed for me. That summer,

Carmen and I became a real couple. We were holding hands and kissing all over New York City: in Central Park, under the Brooklyn bridge, along the Hudson river…everywhere. One day, we were back at my apartment, and my dad and his new girlfriend weren't there. We were alone! This was it! We started kissing on my bed. I wanted to have sex with her so bad! She was completely ready to do it with me but something was stopping me. I didn't know what it was. It must have been fear and anxiety and self-doubt, blocking up all of my positive emotions. I was in love with her, but I was afraid to tell her that I was a virgin. She didn't understand what was wrong with me and I didn't know how to express what I was feeling. In a perfect world I would have told her that I never had sex before. She looked at me frustrated and then gave me a smack, as if to say, "Snap out of it, Taimak!"

Summer ended and Carmen moved back to her neighborhood. I never saw her again. I heard she got married a few years later and had kids. Her sister would tell me that Carmen often asked about me and how I was doing. It was a bittersweet ending. I had had a great time that summer and I felt so good about Carmen, but I just couldn't get past all of the anxiety and doubt that I had inside me. I eventually lost my virginity to an older girl - she was interested in my brother at first, but he didn't give her the time of day - but it just wasn't the same as being with someone who I really cared about. I knew that, if Carmen and I were together, it would've been a whole different ballgame. I was in love with her and I dreamed about recapturing that crazy kind of magical love. All throughout my teenage years, I was struggling to find the confidence to make that happen.

I think that confidence was the most important part of growing up on the streets. The streets were definitely a place where you needed to prove yourself all the time. You had to show that you were tough and that you wouldn't back down from a challenge. The streets could be harsh, and there were plenty of tough guys that were into martial arts who could also make a living with their skills by bouncing at clubs.

When I was 17, I got a job doing security at a nightclub called Bonds International, which was in the center of Times Square. The bouncers there were tough dudes, and I became friends with several of them, including karate black belt Nathan Ingram. The bouncing staff at Bonds was actually pretty tame when compared to the guys at the extremely popular Studio 54; they were known for being violent and edgy, and you couldn't really trust them with a crowd. They didn't always have the most rigorous discipline or code of honor. They were mostly from the hard ghetto, up in the Bronx, and their boss was a tough martial artist named Paul Stewart. Stewart was a tall, athletic, lean, light-skinned guy, and he had all of his bouncer's train in martial arts and wear long braids at the back of their heads with small beads on the bottom of each braid. They were a pretty intimidating sight.

Bonds International, Studio 54, and another club The Paradise Garage, were without a doubt, some of the hottest clubs in New York City in the 80's. Bonds International could hold 6,000 people, and it was quite an otherworldly and unique experience to work there. Before I started working as a bouncer, my high school buddies and I would stand outside clubs like Studio 54 and just watch the ruckus of the huge crowd dying to get inside. There was nothing else like it! It was an event for us every weekend. We would wait for the next celebrity to squeeze through a crowd of wannabes, dying to be selected to step beyond the rope and into the thick atmosphere of neon, cigarette smoke, and throbbing disco music. Every celebrity you could think of was inside these places: Michael Jackson, Diana Ross, Mick Jagger, Andy Warhol, top fashion designers and socialites, and more. You name them, they were there!

I eventually started working as a bouncer at a popular club called 1018, which was originally called The Roxy. It used to be a very popular roller skating rink that opened in 1978 and was then converted into a dance club in the 80's. I was the youngest guy on the bouncing staff, and we were all either martial artists or just tough guys that they hired to keep things under control. There was an older guy who frequented the club who appeared to be in his mid to late 40's. He claimed to be a film producer/director and he told me that he was producing a film called *Delivery Boys*. His name was Ken Handler and he was the son of Barbara and Elliot Handler, founders of Mattel Toys. The famous Ken doll, Barbie's boyfriend, was named after him. Handler told me that he was looking for young men to appear in his new film, especially one for the lead role. He had his eye on me and invited me to do a reading with him at his very expensive three-story house just off of 5th Avenue on 79th St., on the east side of Manhattan. I was excited...what young kid doesn't want to be in the movies?

I went over to his place every day for about a week; I didn't know anything about acting or the movie business, so he basically was trying to let me know the difference between good and bad films and good and bad acting. We watched a few movies and discussed the major roles, and we read a scene or two from the script for *Delivery Boys*. He eventually showed me an excellent film production of *Romeo and Juliet* from 1968, which was directed by Franco Zeffirelli. I had never seen a Shakespearean film before and I thought it was great. He told me that Zeffirelli was gay and that he was having an affair with the young lead actor Leonard Whiting and that was the reason why Leonard's performance was so good. He told me that Leonard never had another successful performance since that movie, and for me to get to that level - if I wanted to deliver a truly great lead performance like the one in *Romeo and Juliet* - he and I would have to develop a very close relationship as well.

That's when I paused and told him that's not what I was interested in. He said, "Well, it's going to be really tough to make it in show business if I didn't understand these things." He gave me a serious look and continued, "Where you are right now, with no experience as an actor, it'll take at least 10 more years to develop that level of talent." I said, "No thank you" and got my things and left, never to see him again...until, ironically, after I was cast in *The Last Dragon*. He was in his car with his family and pulled up to the corner near me, looked out his window and called my name. I looked at him like he was crazy. He must have heard something from one of the other guys at the club about me getting the role in the movie. He yelled out, "Congratulations!" I just walked away.

One of the benefits of working at Bonds and other clubs was that I got to see some of the biggest recording artists of the time doing their thing at the top of their game, and I learned a lot about performing and stage work. I remember one night when I was bouncing at 1018 and the manager asked me to escort a singer to the stage. He brought me over to this young white girl in baggy clothes. She had a cute personality and she was there with two male dancers. At the time, I didn't notice anything out of the ordinary about her, though I recognized the song she sang, "Holiday", from the radio. But this was just the very beginning of her career, and she was about to get huge. While I was walking her to the stage I introduced myself and she said that her name was Madonna. She was just one of many other entertainers who I met at the start of their careers, and it was always really educational to see their performances and to learn about making your first steps into the industry. Somewhere down inside, I knew that I would eventually get my turn.

While I was bouncing at these clubs, I started to open up a bit more and I met a lot of different girls. I felt kind of like the Nutty Professor; I was still shy and didn't have much confidence, but the clubs had music, drinks, flashing lights, and a dark, sultry atmosphere that let me completely cut loose. I felt free because there were so many distractions around me. My friends and I were always at these clubs, partying and meeting girls, competing to see how many girls we could kiss in one night. My friend Richie and I used to hold up our fingers and signal to each other to show how many girls we had kissed - it was a blast! We felt like young Valentinos! I danced with a different girl every night, and we would always find a secluded spot in the club to make out. I would often get their numbers and they would ask me to meet them during the day, but I was usually too afraid to act on it. It was like I had a different persona and confidence level when I was in the club, and all of it disappeared once I stepped outside. I still had a lot of things I needed to work on and a lot of growing that I needed to do.

I knew that if I wanted to be a great entertainer and creative talent, I would have to get over my shyness and find my confidence. When you're an entertainer, you've got to be ready to bare everything for your audience…sometimes literally. For instance, every once in a while, the promoter of Bonds would come up with something to keep the crowd entertained. One day, the promoter had the idea that all of the security guys should do a strip performance. They chose about ten of us for the performance and I would be one of them. I didn't really want to do it, but the other guys were making me laugh and they egged me on. I had to agree! It was one of the scariest things I ever did. I would've rather been in a kickboxing match. The night of the performance, we were all backstage putting oil on our bodies and getting into our speedos. Some of the guys did stripping on the side to make some extra money, so they were in G-strings. We were all laughing and having a good time as we got ready to go out. Before long, the music was pumping and the lights started spinning. I couldn't believe I was going to do it! They had roped off a huge area of the dance floor; it was like an airport terminal or something. Each guy went out, one at a time, and worked the crowd. When it was my turn, the whole experience was just a total blur. I remember girls screaming and not much else. I returned backstage as soon as I could, and the older guys said, "You should have taken more time out there!" and, "Hey, did you have fun? They liked you!" I can't say it was too fun, really…I had no problem doing this sort of thing in front of one girlfriend, but there must have been at least 500 people out there!

I really didn't have the confidence that I needed to relax and open up. As I mentioned earlier, one of the major reasons for my low self-confidence was the bullying that I got from my brother. He was always doing something to pick on me and he was bigger and older, so he could always beat me in a fight. He also had a serious mean streak about him, and he would lash out for really small and petty things. I used to hate going home, especially if I knew that our dad wouldn't be there. At the same time, I always looked up to him. He was the smartest kid in every school he attended and I guess that also played into my insecurities. I never felt I was as good as my brother. These feelings really drove me to become better at everything I did. I unconsciously seemed to compare myself to him a lot. I always wanted to be as smart as him, to be as big and strong as him. He could have been a sort of mentor or at least a friend. As it was, he was like an obstacle that kept me from being fully happy.

When I was about 16, however, everything came to a head. My brother and I got into an argument in the hallway of our building. I don't even remember what the fight was about but it grew physical. By this time, I was pretty good with martial arts, and I had grown a lot stronger and more disciplined. I'd been continually studying techniques and getting better as the years went on. My brother, on the other hand, had stopped studying martial arts when we were little kids. As we argued and pushed each other around, I gave him a kick in the stomach that knocked him into the neighbor's door.

I yelled, "you'll never put your hands on me again!" He looked at me with fear in his eyes and shouted, "You're crazy," and ran away. It was a huge victory for me in my young life. The tables had finally turned after all those years of harassment! I don't think that my brother had ever understood the deep pain that he had caused me for so many years.

After that day, he never put his hands on me again. I don't advocate violence as an answer to any kind of conflict, but sometimes you need to stand up for yourself and assert that you're not going to let someone else control your life. It was an important lesson that would stay with me throughout the rest of my life; you need to stand up, be strong, and learn how to protect yourself and the people you care about. Otherwise, negativity will be able to just steamroll you right over. If you aren't careful, you can allow other people to decide your destiny. If I wanted to be a hero, I needed to stand up for myself and I had to take my destiny into my own hands. When I stood up for myself and prevented my brother from controlling my life and feelings, I felt such a huge surge of confidence and self-respect. I knew that I was on the path to becoming a stronger and more mature person, and I was finally taking my first steps to becoming the hero that I always knew I could be.

Chapter 5 – From Imagination to Reality

"You will not be punished for your anger, you will be punished by your anger."

Buddha

Throughout these early years, I was powered by two things: imagination and martial arts. Imagination was something that was absolutely essential to me, because it gave me the ability to shoot for something higher. You've got to be a dreamer in life. You need imagination to take you out of the mundane realities of that everyday world, full of deadlines and stress. We need to work to see beyond that. We need ambitions that will expand our horizons of what is possible. The other major force that kept me going was martial arts. Whenever I got tired or started to slow down as a kid, martial arts helped me to build up my spirit and confidence. I definitely appreciated the physical, combative side of martial arts, but I really felt more affinity for the spiritual side of things. The combative stuff was more of a front, a chance to show off for other kids or girls. It was the spirituality of martial arts that truly connected with me. I had a real yearning for peace and harmony, because I came from such a chaotic upbringing.

I learned a lot about spirituality and harmony from all those great Shaw Brothers kung fu movies. I saw the way that the heroes in those films always attained some fantastic level of victory. They wouldn't just defeat the big bad guy - they would also display great growth to gain wisdom in the end. The Shaolin monks were often spewing wisdom and the training was always intense. The monks always seemed to be peaceful and they had a lot of serenity and inner peace. I had so much energy growing up, but I didn't like the violence that I grew up around; I wanted to learn to be peaceful, just like the Shaolin monks. I also really enjoyed the TV series *Kung Fu*. Despite the fact that Bruce Lee would have been incredible as the show's star (he was originally supposed to be the lead, but they hired David Carradine instead), I still liked Carradine's performance. I especially connected with the show's overall message that there was a deeper side to martial arts that was about much more than just combat. I really wanted to incorporate that sort of philosophy into my own life.

I started reading a lot more, and I found a book called *Creative Visualization* by Shakti Gawain. The basic concept of the book was that you could use your imagination to visualize what you wanted out of life, and that this would help you to achieve your goals. This sort of thinking helped me to create a vision of what I really wanted, and I used it to improve my training. I imagined that I was a Shaolin monk, undergoing rigorous training in the legendary training chambers of a Shaolin Temple. I visualized myself as a serene master, overcoming the mental and spiritual struggles that were raging inside of me and using these struggles to grow as a person.

Before I read about creative visualization and started to recognize my own yearning for a more harmonious life, I was still fighting in martial arts tournaments and trying to vent all of my emotions and pent-up energy. I eventually got the chance to fight for the New York kickboxing title at the Jerome Boxing Gym in the Bronx! I was excited and anxious, but I trained hard and I knew that I had what it took to go all the way. I remember the fight like it was yesterday...

I stood in the ring, feeling warmed up and filled with nervous energy. My opponent started to stalk out of the locker room. I liked the guy and he was really friendly to me, but he definitely thought that he was hot shit, like Stallone, Bruce Lee, and Roy O'Neal from *Superfly* all rolled into one dude. His entrance music blared over the speakers and I'm pretty sure the song was "Eye of the Tiger". If I can't remember the song, it's because I had tuned out almost everything around me: I was in the zone, just one sweaty, hyped-up ball of energy that was ready to burst.

I didn't even notice when he finally entered the ring. When I snapped back to my senses, he was standing in the middle of the ring, sizing me up with a sly little smile on his face. Yeah, I liked the guy, but he was way too cocky! He thought that he had this all figured out. I was gonna let him believe that for a few minutes.

We both bounced up to the center of the ring and touched gloves. I had planned to sit back and just let him blow off some steam, but he really did come at me like a freight train! I was going to have to put in some serious work. I ducked a few strikes and went in for a few of my own, and we were toe-to-toe. I was worried for a moment – I knew that, if we went on like this, either one of us could get knocked out at any second – but I don't think that he realized that. If he did realize it, he didn't care too much. I kept hearing him mutter, "Yeah, yeah, yeah!" under his breath. He was on a rampage and probably didn't even know what he was punching at!

I backed up and waited a bit until I saw my chance. I kicked my leg back and prepared to slash it out. I felt my calf touch the ropes, and it was like my leg was an arrow, ready to shoot off. He saw my move and started to block it - but that was just what I wanted. I threw a right hand that landed perfectly on his chin, and he was knocked out cold. I was ecstatic! I threw a back flip into the center of the ring and jumped all over the place like I was nuts. My coach and the cut man grabbed me and we all hugged. It was an incredible feeling...I was the champion!

Even with this sort of success, though, I felt kind of lost. It would still be a little while before I got in touch with the spiritual side of martial arts, and I didn't have any direction or plan for what I should do next.

Shortly after I turned 18, there was a lot of talk in the competitive martial arts scene about an upcoming martial arts film that was being cast locally. A Motown music mogul was the producer, and there were casting calls for the movie in different cities around the country. It was a big deal! Every young guy who could throw a kick wanted to audition for it. Ron Van Clief called me about it and told me that I would be perfect for the lead role. I was a bit surprised at first - what sort of martial arts movie was this going to be if they were going to shoot it in New York and were open to casting a black kid like me? This was going to be very different from the kung fu flicks that I was accustomed to. I loved it whenever I saw people of color in kung fu movies, and I looked up to stars like Ron and Jim Kelly - now I was going to get the chance to be one of those guys!

A few years before this, when I was in junior high school, I lived around the corner from the High School for Performing Arts, and it was my dream to get into that school and act. I would look out my window and watch all the actors and dancers. They were going through the motions and just being themselves, and all of the students looked so expressive and free. I wanted to be part of it! I didn't tell anybody, but I went to audition for that school when I was 13. I got a monologue collection from a bookstore and memorized it. Unfortunately, I was so nervous at the audition that I froze up and didn't perform well. Needless to say, I didn't make it into the school. I was devastated at the time, but now I would have a second chance to make things right and reach for my dreams.

Of course, I had no idea how to read for an audition and didn't know anything about how to do a cold reading. When I got more information about this new movie, which was called *The Last Dragon*, I realized that I also didn't really understand the role. The lead character's name was Bruce Leroy, and he spoke without contractions...what was this role? What was I supposed to get across to the audience with my performance? Regardless of my confusion, I was able to get a date for an audition through Lester Wilson, one of our family friends, who happened to be one of the dance choreographers for the film.

I walked into the audition and didn't know what to expect other than the fact that I would be performing for a very powerful casting director named Jeremy Ritzer. He was one half of the well-known Feurer and Ritzer Casting Agency that cast many television shows, movies, and Broadway productions. I was a little nervous, yet confident and excited. I thought that I was going to get the opportunity to show my martial arts movements and that would awe them enough to give me the role. I went upstairs and saw a few actors sitting in chairs outside the office door. Jeremy came out, asked me to sign in and went back into the office. He was professional, but also very kind. This whole set up made me feel like a fish out of water because I had never auditioned for anything except for the High School for the Performing Arts - unless you count the stint with that so-called film producer.

Soon after, Jeremy reappeared and gave me something called "sides". Sides are dialogue scenes from a script/screenplay that casting directors use in auditions. He told me to take my time, look over the scene, and then knock on the door when I was ready to read for him. If I felt like a fish out of water before, I now felt like I was about to flop about on dry land. I looked at the scene and it was just about some guy with a coolie hat. It made no sense to me. However, I knew that I had to go in the room and show off my skills so I just knocked on the door and he let me in.

I noticed right away that there was no room to throw kicks or perform any martial arts moves. I was totally blindsided...I realized that all we were going to do was just the scene from the side. We were doing a cold reading, which I had never done before. Jeremy asked me to begin reading and I gave it a try, but I completely failed and performed terribly. I wasn't a professional actor and had no understanding on how to break down the scene for an audition. Jeremy stopped me and told me that I needed to do more work on it and that maybe I could come again another time. My whole performance was lukewarm at best. I obviously didn't get the part, and I was left going home with my tail between my legs.

Soon afterwards, my dad offered a job for me and my best friend Richie. We were going to drive down to Coconut Grove in Miami, Florida to clean rooftops. Richie and I thought it was a great idea! It was getting cold in New York and we would really enjoy the warm weather in Miami. Richie and I were also happy because we would get the chance to chase after all the Miami girls on the beach. Richie and I packed for our trip, got into my dad's van, and we began our road trip to Florida. On the way there, my dad wanted to work on *The Last Dragon* with me. He would always ask me to break out the script so that we could work on a scene. He wanted me to really get into the character. I didn't mind at first, but I got tired of it pretty quickly; my dad was really aggressive and almost violent when he gave me notes, and it was really unpleasant. Every time I did something that he didn't think was right, he whacked me over the head and said, "No, that's not how it goes. Don't you understand?" In these moments, Richie wouldn't say anything, but I could tell that he felt bad for me. I knew it wasn't my dad's intention, but he was approaching me with a lot of intensity and aggressive energy.

There was no way that I could perform well under those circumstances. Even though we eventually reached Florida with all its sunshine, I was in a bad mood. We got out of the car and started taking our things into the place where we were staying. I told Richie, "I don't think I want the role anymore, maybe it's just not for me." He stopped and looked at me, and he said something that I'll never forget, "If there is a God on Earth, that role was written for you." I paused for a second, taking it in, and then we walked inside and got unpacking. What he said really struck me and it motivated me to keep working on my performance. I just made sure to do it alone or once in a while when I was goofing around with Richie. We spent the rest of our time in Florida just cracking jokes and laughing, having a good time. We cleaned rooftops during the day and had fun in Coconut Grove in the night. A month or so went by and we eventually headed back to New York.

When we got back, I immediately went back to the casting office for the film. I knocked on the front door and Jeremy Ritzer opened it. He was less than excited and had a look on his face like, "Oh, you again." I didn't let that bother me - I was determined to have another chance and to make the most of it. He let me in and I sat down, but he remained standing and kept going on about his business, moving papers around and doing little things in his office as if I wasn't there. He eventually started reading the scene with me, but he was doing it in a really half-baked, lazy way. I didn't let that stop me, though...I gave it my all. After a few seconds, he must've noticed that my reading was different and much improved. He finally sat down and gave me his full attention and we continued reading for another minute. It was obvious that I had gotten much better and he was clearly impressed. He stopped the reading and made a phone call to the production office. Next thing I knew, he gave me the address to the production office and told me to get over there now and meet the producer. It was somewhere between 49th Street and 52nd Street, all the way on the west side by 11th Avenue. I rushed over there, filled with excitement!

When I got there, I met the producer, Rupert Hitzig and the writer, Louis Venosta. They interviewed me and asked me to read one of the scenes several times. I could tell that things were going well. They had me meet the director's wife so that she could read a scene with me (this later became an actual scene in the movie where I go to Laura Charles's apartment to get my belt buckle). The director was Michael Schultz and his wife was named Gloria. She was really sweet and worked with me on the scene and gave me some great advice on my performance. After continuing to meet with everyone and working on it for a few days, they thought I was ready to meet Berry Gordy, the film's executive producer and chairman of Motown Records. I was going to perform this scene for one of the most influential men in the entertainment business! Everything was moving so fast that I didn't quite understand the immensity of what was going on. Berry was a true star-maker - he developed the careers of Michael Jackson, Diana Ross, Stevie Wonder, Marvin Gaye, and so many other huge pop stars. *The Last Dragon* was going to be Berry's chance to carry over his musical success into the world of movies.

While I waited at the production office for Berry to show up, Gloria helped me prepare for my reading. I had practiced with her just a few days earlier, but it was important for me to get back into a good dramatic rhythm. We kept going over lines until the doors opened and Berry (or, as everyone called him, The Chairman) walked in with his entourage. It was a very interesting bunch of people. He was wearing shades and was about 60 years-old. He had a young Asian girlfriend with hair that touched the ground. They all sat down and didn't say anything.

When Gloria and I started to perform the scene, I looked at The Chairman out of the corner of my eye. I noticed that he was intensely studying what we were doing. He started to roll his tongue around in his mouth - it was a signature thing that he was known for by people who worked with him, and it was a sign that he was really into something. After we were done, he jumped out of his seat and clapped his hands and applauded. I could tell he was ready for business, and it felt great! They offered me the role, and I was ecstatic. Everything was moving so fast! I didn't even have time to let too many people know that I was about to land the lead role in one of the biggest martial arts movies made in the past 10 years...a film that would actually star a kid of color! It was a huge production: a romantic action/comedy directed by the extremely respected filmmaker, Michael Schultz, produced by the legendary Berry Gordy, in partnership with the major movie studio Tri-Star Films. I was just a kid from New York with dreams of being a martial arts action hero, and I had never anticipated that I would achieve this level of success at such an early age.

I had a rough time negotiating the contract, though. I had hired an attorney, a friend of a friend, but the studio didn't want to work with him. It's always a red flag when a production doesn't want to work with your attorney or agent. My attorney told me, "It's a horrible deal. They really do want you for the lead role...they even fired somebody else, even though they had already unofficially promised the role to him. After they saw you, they felt that you were the only one who could do it. But they're being cheap and they only want to give you scale pay." If they were going to pay me scale, this would mean that they were only going to pay me the bare minimum that you can pay anybody under the Screen Actors Guild union rules.

I was really confused about what to do. I didn't know anything about the business or what actors got paid. There was no Internet, so I couldn't just Google around and do some research. I was told that actors in lead roles got anywhere from $75,000 and up, but obviously I didn't have any experience and didn't want to give them a hard time and risk losing the part. I now know that they would have given me more money if I had held my ground. But since I was naïve and innocent at the time, I decided to sign. I agreed to do the role for $30,000; it was a lot of money to me at the time, but I wish I had asked for more. It would take me many years to finally learn certain lessons about the film industry and how to prevent myself from being exploited, but at the time I was only a kid. In the meantime, I was just excited that I was about to become an action hero!

Chapter 6 – The Dragon's Path

*"We are continually faced by great opportunities
brilliantly disguised as insoluble problems."*

Anonymous

When you're about to step into the ring, every muscle in your body just tingles with anticipation. It's like you enter into a sort of higher state of being - you're surrounded by energy and time starts to move at a totally different pace. That's exactly how it felt when I got cast in *The Last Dragon*. It seemed to all happen in an instant and I had a lot of work to do to get prepared for the role. The day I met the rest of the cast was really amazing! Everyone in the room had so much talent and charisma. I knew I was involved with something special. The film's production schedule was really fast. We rehearsed for a bit and started shooting only a few weeks later.

Here is the basic plot of *The Last Dragon*: my character, Bruce Leroy, is a young martial artist who looks up to Bruce Lee (the perfect role for me, right?). Leroy wants to become a great martial arts hero. His master explains that he has touched upon the final level of martial arts known as "The Last Dragon", and that he must try and achieve a higher level of physical and mental potential; a state of being called "The Glow", where the martial artists' ability to concentrate mystical energy will cause their whole body to shine and glow. In order to achieve The Glow, Leroy sets off on a journey to find Master Sum Dum Goy who can help unlock this power. Along his journey, Leroy is challenged by the villainous Sho'nuff, the self-proclaimed Shogun of Harlem. Leroy needs to protect his friends from Sho'nuff, all the while learning to activate The Glow. On top of all of this action, the film had a soundtrack that was produced by Berry Gordy's legendary Motown Records, with songs by Stevie Wonder, Willie Hutch, and the song, "Rhythm of the Night" by DeBarge, which was a huge hit.

The Last Dragon and the experiences that I had while making the movie were such a transformative and life-changing time for me. I'll never forget the experiences that I had or the people I met. This chapter is about my relationships with the cast and crew of the film. Everyone who worked on the film was unique and really special in their own way, and they all left their own stamp on the finished product and on me.

Denise Matthews, best known to the world by her stage name Vanity, is well-remembered by every young guy who saw the movie. She played Laura Charles, the film's heroine, and all the men on the set turned into puppy dogs when she walked into the room. Denise and I met during pre-production, and I certainly thought she was beautiful. She was already a bit of a star - she was the lead singer of a female trio group called Vanity 6, and had a hit song called "Nasty Girl". She had even dated Prince. She was most definitely a very memorable part of the film. Many women over the years have imitated Denise's attitude and mannerisms from the movie. I wish I had a dollar for every woman who has copied her hand movements and slyly said, "Never say never," which was a great moment in the film. Moments like these make me realize that this movie really struck the hearts of so many people.

While we were in rehearsal, Denise and I went on a few dinner dates. We discussed her moving to New York, but I sensed that that she was wrapped up in the fluff of Hollywood. She was an intelligent woman; unlike me, she knew her value as a commodity in the entertainment business and she knew how to market her sex appeal. But she didn't really seem to understand her value as a person. Based on what she was telling me, she didn't appear to be serious about acting - I felt that she enjoyed the job more for the glamour rather than the art. I felt that she was a little too eager for stardom and she needed to be more grounded. I tried to convince her to come out to New York and join the theatre scene to really develop her craft, away from the glamour and distractions of Hollywood. She wasn't too interested though, and wanted to remain on the west coast.

But hey, what did I know? I was only 19. Denise was a little older than me and already had a hit song out. This was my first acting gig, and I wasn't a seasoned performer by any means, and I needed a lot of guidance myself. We actually both needed really good managers who could help us build our careers and who could navigate us through the difficult terrain of the film industry, which can really take an emotional and psychological toll on you.

Once we started filming, Denise and I became more focused on our work, but we also started to drift apart. I felt that she behaved like a *prima donna* and I was just over it. I had no intention of being a puppy dog like the rest of the guys on the set. We didn't communicate very well, and we barely even spoke to each other for the first week. When I got really annoyed with her, Berry or my acting coach would take me to the side and explain to me how to deal with the tense situation. The friction between us was over silly stuff. I wanted to stand up in a scene but she wanted me to sit down. It was small little things like that. She wanted to screw with me a bit and it was definitely working. I remember Berry pulling me to the side one day and saying, "Taimak, if you think Denise is a pain in the ass, wait until you work with some *real* pain in the ass people!" He was definitely right about that.

Denise and I continued to have a strained working relationship, all the way up to our kissing scene. I decided that I was going to set things straight when we kissed and I put a lot of energy into the moment. Michael and Berry loved it, and Denise and I were pretty much fine afterwards. It's funny how a little love can break the tension. In the end, Denise had a different lifestyle than me; she was into the Hollywood party scene and I wasn't. She had a fun spirit, but at the time she was a bit too Hollywood for my east-coast personality.

One of the interesting things about Denise was that she put a lot of focus on managing her personal brand. We didn't quite have the concept of "branding" back then, so she was definitely ahead of the curve. She knew how she wanted people to see her and was extremely attuned to how she presented herself to the world. She made a conscious choice to do *The Last Dragon* so that she could put a different image of herself in front of audiences. Before this film, when she was involved with Prince and released the "Nasty

Girls" song, she had a sexualized image. By starring in *The Last Dragon*, she could present herself as a more wholesome and family friendly star. It was a smart decision.

At some point, I met up with Denise and her sister Patricia (who was a cool girl, also attractive and more grounded than Denise) at a casino. I can't remember if Denise was performing at the casino or what the occasion was, but her mom was there too. Denise was constantly jumping around and I didn't understand what was going on with her, but I later found out that she had developed a cocaine addiction. We didn't talk again until the late 80's, but it was a very awkward interaction on the phone. Drug abuse can change people so much that you can barely recognize them, or make it impossible to connect with them like you once did. Denise's continued abuse of cocaine would eventually lead to an overdose and near fatal renal failure. She turned to religion as a born again Christian so she could leave her addiction behind and solve her other issues. It worked for her and she even became an evangelist for Christianity. She wrote a very interesting book about her experiences called *Blame It on Vanity*.

In the end, though, Denise's story is somewhat tragic. While I was writing this book, Denise passed away at the young age of 57 from renal failure, caused by years of drug use. She went through a lot of struggles in Hollywood and the entertainment industry wasn't easy on her. However, she had the courage to be honest about her problems in life and she shared them with the world so that she could ultimately live a life of service. Nobody's perfect and she did the best she could under the circumstances. She reached out to me several times over the past twenty years but I didn't always know how to help her deal with her struggles. I didn't have the proper knowledge or maturity to help her through these difficulties. It's probably for the best that I wasn't lecturing her. What she needed was unconditional love, and not a lecture. She found the help she needed through religion, and I was happy that she was able to achieve a certain amount of inner peace.

I also formed an interesting mentor-student relationship with Julius Carry, who played Sho'nuff, the Shogun of Harlem. He was a hilarious guy, and we had a lot of chemistry together. He knew that I liked him a lot but he felt that we were becoming too friendly with each other. You see, Julius was a serious actor and he knew that there had to be a sense of antagonism between us because he was my nemesis in the film. His concern was that our relationship would be too positive and there wouldn't be enough tension on the screen. To solve this issue, he used to constantly pick on me and create fights. For instance, between takes, Julius would walk around the set and stay in character. Everyone would laugh at his antics. He didn't mind everyone else laughing...but I wasn't allowed to. He would get really offended by my laughter, approach me, and start needling me about whatever he could. He teased me about my outfit or about my performance, and he even got one of the set choreographers (knowing that I didn't like the guy) to mock me as much as he could. I would get pretty heated and chase Julius around the set to try and kick his ass. The funny thing is that he was about 6'7 and I'm 5'11. Nevertheless, he ran away like a little kid when I chased him and people had to stop me and calm me down.

I figured out later that it was all a game for him so that he could create tension between us. If you look at his work in *The Last Dragon*, you might think that Julius was just clowning, but I believe that he brilliantly crafted his role and very specifically delivered a memorable performance that was unique and exciting. He had a lot of acting experience, including Shakespearean plays, and he had real acting chops.

Julius was a nice guy, but he was living in the west coast and was 12 years-older than me, so it was difficult for us to have a lasting friendship. There was no social media back then and communication wasn't the same as it is today. He definitely had some successes after *The Last Dragon*, including projects like *The Adventures of Brisco County, Jr.*, *Murphy Brown* and other things. Even though I wasn't landing many roles myself, I was very happy to turn on the tube and see him doing his thing. I wish that I could have gotten to know him better. At the time, I was just a kid and at a very different stage in my life and career, but I know that we would be good friends if he were still alive today.

It's always difficult to look back and think about the relationships and friendships that you missed out on in life. For instance, Leo O'Brien, who played my little brother in the film, was something else. I thought he was a 50 year-old man in a 10 year-old kid's body, and he made me laugh so much. I eventually found out he was older than I thought (he was 14, not 10)...for a long time, I just thought he was a little kid who was way too wise for his age. Leo's brother was Master G from The Sugar Hill Gang, one of the pioneers of hip-hop, so he was already used to being in the performance world.

Goofing around on the set of "The Last Dragon". Glen Eaton and Leo in the background.

We had good chemistry from the first moment we began working together. The producers had me sit down in an office with a bunch of different kids who would potentially play my brother, and Leo and I clicked right away. He didn't really look like me, but he was such a talented and funny young guy that he easily got the part. The whole experience of *The Last Dragon* was unfortunately sort of a letdown for Leo. He had such huge hopes for what the movie could do for his career, but he didn't ultimately get the success that he wanted. I was young at the time, but Leo I was even younger and I think he had even higher expectations than I did (which was pretty damn high, because my expectations were through the roof).

I didn't see Leo until 2011, when I heard about an incident where he got shot in Harlem. Leo said that he didn't know why the guy shot him, but the shooter was someone who he knew. I was obviously upset to hear this news and I went to see him in the hospital. As soon as Leo saw me, he got really excited and started talking his head off. His stomach had been cut open to take the bullets out, but he was still full of energy! I was thirsty and asked where I could get some water. He said, "Don't worry T, I'll get it for you." He got up and I told him to get his butt back into bed, but he kept on insisting, "I got this!" He yelled for the nurses as he stormed through the hallway, all hyped up on painkillers. He was certainly a character.

I had just written a short film called *I've Seen Things* and I thought it would be good for us to work together again. I wanted to give his spirits a boost, so I asked if he would be interested in working with me. He said, "Hell yeah." I was really looking forward to it! He rehearsed with me and a few of the other cast members and he hadn't lost a beat; his acting skills were still sharp as ever and he still had that unique sense of wise cracking, sarcastic humor everyone loved so much in *The Last Dragon*. We had a few more rehearsals, and things seemed to be going well. One morning, I was awakened by a phone call at around 5:00 AM. I picked up the phone and it was Leo's son. I had never met him before, so it was unexpected for me to get a call from him. I knew something was wrong. He said, "Hello Taimak, I'm Leo's son. My dad died last night." It was a shock. Julius Carry had just recently died, and now Leo was gone too. I put my project on hold after his death.

In the end, Leo didn't have an easy life. It's very difficult, and not very fun to be a child star. There are all the expectations and insecurities one has to ordinarily deal with as a little kid or as a teenager, and now all of a sudden your life is open for everyone else to pick apart and analyze. It's not a normal childhood. I don't think he ever felt whole and complete. I wish that I had had the foresight to get to know Leo and Julius better before they died. I would have gotten them both together with me to tour around the country, signing autographs and meeting the fans at conventions. It would have been a blast.

Chazz Palminteri was also in the film, and it was only his second role. Chazz played the henchman of one of the movie's villains, Eddie Arcadian. It was a lot of fun to work with him; he was one of the few guys who did a lot of goofing around on the set, just wisecracking and playing jokes. He really kept me laughing. Sal Russo, who played another one of the henchmen, was another guy who was always cracking me up with his comments. Chazz and Sal kept my energy and spirits up whenever they were around, which was really essential to me...the production was exhausting, and some of the tougher, longer days could really take their toll on you. Sal was Berry's limo driver, which was how he got that small role in the film. The fact that Sal got a role in the movie wasn't surprising: in a way, the whole film was a family affair, and a lot of people were related or connected to each other. Michael Schultz cast his kids in a couple of small parts and his wife, Gloria, was a help to me as an informal acting coach. Denise's hairdresser in the film was even her actual hairdresser! He was a really funny guy, and everybody thought he was perfect to play that part (and he definitely was).

Glen Eaton, who played Johnny Yu, was actually Berry's girlfriend's brother. He wasn't just hired because of nepotism, he had true talent. Glen had already done some work in California. Glen and I got to know each other a little bit, because the production put us up in an apartment together during filming. We were both very focused and had a lot of work to do, but every once in a while we found the time to go running together in Central Park. Once shooting wrapped, I took Glen out to a bunch of clubs, including Studio 54. What was going out for a night of fun in New York City, 1984, if you didn't go to Studio 54, right? Glen loved it and we had a great time. Unfortunately, I didn't see him much after that. I ran into him years later in the 90's in Los Angeles. He was no longer acting and was working in an ice cream parlor. It was disheartening to see him there, but I had to respect where he was at in life. You have to eat, make a living, and provide for your family. Unfortunately, a lot of actors aren't able to do the thing that they love to do, but that's life. It's tough to make it in the entertainment world, and talent sometimes isn't enough.

While we were filming, I didn't go to my parents too much for guidance. I was too busy to get into what was happening- not just that I was appearing in it, but starring in it! My childhood relationship with them was strained and confusing and when it came to business decisions, I didn't always see them as the most experienced, although they had been around artists a lot, the business was a different animal. I basically chose to learn things on my own during those years, which wasn't a good idea, because it's a period where you really need to have proper guidance. In their place, many people on the set of the film mentored me. Berry especially gave me a lot of guidance and coaching. He really made me believe in myself. I also formed a fantastic relationship with my acting coach, Richard Fancy. He had me do "emotional memory" exercises so that I could get a deeper understanding of my emotional inner being. To be honest, I didn't always see how these exercises connected with what I specifically had to do in my scenes. However, the specifics didn't matter; even if I wasn't always sure how his exercises were related to my work, he was *there* for me during the shooting of the movie.

While I worked on the film, my confidence began to grow, and I got together with a girl from the crew. She was older than I was - I was 19 and she was 27. Her name was Carla Brothers and she would later appear in a movie called *The 5 Heartbeats*. She was laidback, mature, and down-to-earth, which was just what I needed. We dated seriously, and we continued to see each other after the filming was complete. Carla was a trained actress who graduated from the NYU Acting Program and studied directly with the master teacher, Lee Strasberg. She helped me to understand that acting was a craft that I had to learn and she inspired me to read books on the subject of acting. We had a lot of fun together and I learned a lot, but I was too young and immature to get too serious with one girl. I was already becoming a celebrity, and girls were always coming onto me, just about everywhere I went. We eventually broke up but we remained very friendly. I think we both knew that it couldn't last. I didn't know who I was yet and I needed time to learn.

Not all of my relationships on the set were positive, of course. One of the choreographers instigated a lot of problems with me, which created a very negative environment. For instance, it was important in my role to move like Bruce Lee, since Bruce Leroy idolized him. I tried my best to get Bruce's movements down, but the choreographer would always step in and scream, "No man, like this!" He constantly lectured me about my personality, and how I needed to be open in my scenes and do better. I never felt any love from him, but rather bitterness, hatred, and perhaps even jealousy -- it was no secret that he had actually auditioned for the role of Bruce Leroy, and he was perhaps unhappy that he did not get it. Thankfully, I had Ron Van Clief there with me, who I trusted. Ron had been hired as one of the fight team choreographers. Ernie Reyes Sr. was another one of the choreographers, and he was a real gentleman and an awesome person.

I didn't let negative moments like that get me down, and I did my best to embrace the many other great relationships that I made on the set. At the end of the day, I was still just a 19 year-old kid. When we shot the scene where my master explains my journey to me, I really feel it was a case of art imitating life. So much of what my master was saying was actually true for me at the time, and I embraced it as if I really was the character. It was as if he was speaking directly to me and referencing all of the things that I had already been through: "Confusion is a part of life, as are vengeance, fear and love. All facets must be embraced..." These lines spoke to me and I felt a very deep connection with Bruce Leroy. I had to act like a confused 19 year-old in that scene, and it wasn't difficult - I actually was a confused 19 year-old! I really experienced those emotions and I cried real tears.

Chapter 7 - Filming *The Last Dragon*

"We think this isn't it, but it is...cherish every moment with every inch of your being." - Taimak

I have many stories from the filming of *The Last Dragon*. When I watch the movie all these years later, I notice how focused I was during the entire shoot. Between the crazy and hilarious costumes, the energy of all the cast and crew, and all the wild characters popping in and off the set, I had to work hard to stay focused on my lines and Michael Shultz's direction. Michael was a true professional and a great mentor who brought out the best in me. He knew how to turn my inexperience into an asset, and to keep things sharp and simple.

I still remember my first day of shooting. It was an interior shot, and we were filming in the tight hallway of an apartment. The producers wouldn't allow anyone on the set unless they were actually in a particular shot, because the space was just too small and things would get too cluttered. I was waiting around behind the scenes and I had no idea what they were shooting or how things looked. When it was finally my turn to get in front of the camera, I walked onto the set and I was stunned. There were so many crew members running around and preparing things: camera assistants, camera operators, electricians, set decorators, film loaders, hair and makeup staff, lighting technicians, and countless others. It was like the population of a small city was crammed into this little space. I realized then that I was working on a big budget film and that this was a huge production. Yesterday, I had never been in a movie before, and now

I was being asked to star in one of the biggest martial arts movies ever made.

When I stood in front of the camera for the first time, I could almost sense the camera lens as it focused in on me. I felt like I was at home and I was totally relaxed. I knew that this was the beginning of something special. When we finished shooting the scene, I was charged up with energy and I felt like I could take on the world. It was a really intense feeling, like a natural high. After we broke for lunch, I had to go for a run in Central Park so that I could clear my head. I had to wonder whether every scene was going to be that intense. I needed to take it easy and keep calm, or else I was going to give myself a heart attack!

There were definitely times when the shoot was almost too overwhelming to comprehend. This was especially true of the scene that we shot in a grungy movie theater on 42nd Street. In a way, I felt very much at home in this scene; I spent so much time hanging out in theaters like this watching my favorite martial arts heroes, including the very theater we were shooting in. On the other hand, dozens of people filled this little space, and it was truly chaotic, in a beautiful, crazy sort of way. Many of these people were young aspiring actors while others were just characters that the casting people found who looked like they could be off the streets or out of a dojo. Everyone was super excited to be part of this movie - it was a chance to be seen, to get their 15 minutes of fame, or maybe even a line or two that they could add to their acting reel.

There were a lot of characters on the set that day. The casting people really chose their extras well. They had a great understanding of the type of characters that would frequent 42nd St. movie theaters, real oddball types of people, and that's exactly what we got in this scene. I remember a kid named Airborne, who was a member of a successful break dancing crew called The Dynamic Breakers (my mom actually managed the group when she came back to the U.S.). There were also these two guys who everyone on the set was laughing about (they were big dudes, though, so nobody really laughed in their faces). One of them had this pink tank top that only came down to his navel, and he looked rather silly. He kept trying to pull it down so that nobody would laugh at him. These big guys were pretty tough, and there was one incident where they aggressively rushed through the set and accidentally knocked over one of the extras, a transgender girl. They broke her ribs and we had to pause the filming to get her some medical help. It was important for the film and the scene to have a transgender extra on the set. These grindhouse theaters were a refuge for everyone who felt like they were an outcast from society, and you could always meet all sorts of people from every walk of life.

I filmed so many other crazy scenes, but I barely had time to catch my breath and think about what I was doing. The scene where I had to dodge all of those arrows was especially wild and overwhelming. Those arrows came at me really fast, but I was game and enjoyed the challenge. I was really showing off and chopping at them as much as I could. The arrows were lightweight and dulled, but they were real! If one of them had caught me in the eye, I would have been blinded. They took every precaution to keep me safe, though. The archery master shot at my chest, not my face, and the arrows were placed in a special protective shaft. It was one of the early scenes on the schedule and it wouldn't have been a good thing if I got injured in the very beginning of production.

I didn't really know what I was doing in these action scenes. I was just going with the flow and using my natural athleticism and martial arts training to get me through them. I was running on my instincts. In a way, though, I had been preparing for this moment my entire life. I was finally a real action hero, just like the Shaw Brothers characters who I idolized. When I filmed these scenes, I felt like Bruce Lee or Sonny Chiba, putting myself into the action and facing danger. It was a thrilling feeling, and I think that energy shows up on the screen. I had fun, but I also feel that I didn't appreciate the moment as much as I should have, or as much as I would have if I was older. There were too many distractions for me to really take everything in and understand the uniqueness of what I was doing.

I learned a lot from the other actors on the set. There were times when I would just stand off to the side and watch them perform. I was especially impressed with Christopher Murney and Faith Prince, who played Eddie Arcadian and Angela Viracco. Chris and Faith were very focused and they really sold their relationship. Michael Schultz worked with them a lot so that they could fully bring out the dynamic between their characters. When I watched the three of them going over a scene and discussing the different performance choices, I really felt that I was watching a team of brilliant artists at work. Michael had a special way of connecting with actors and helping them to achieve the best and most interesting performance. I'll also never forget shooting the scene where Sho'nuff and his gang kick down the doors and make their challenge. Julius and the actors who played his gang had stayed in character throughout their entire time on the set, and everyone was intimidated by them. No one had to act like they were scared - we really were, even the crew members! Julius had a way of capturing your attention that I'll never forget, and his performance really taught me how to grab an audience.

The whole shoot was truly an education in filmmaking. For instance, a lot of fans love the moment where I enter the Chinese guys' place looking for the Master. I was wearing a white fedora style hat and big black shades, hoping they wouldn't recognize me. I added a bit of swagger in my walk. While I was doing that scene, a lot of the crew laughed and just ate it up. The performance was pretty charming, if I say so myself. The scene looks effortless, but it actually took a lot of work to get right. We shot the scene a few times, but it just wasn't popping like it should. It wasn't as funny or entertaining as it could be. Michael and Berry sat down and reworked the whole thing, making sure that the dialogue really snapped and the whole scene was more warm and exciting. When they were done, it was a completely different scene. The other actors and I had to memorize a bunch of new lines, right there on the spot. It was definitely an important thing to learn about the way films are made - anything and everything can change at a moment's notice.

The spontaneous quality of moviemaking was exciting to me. I had to think on my feet and be ready for anything. I quickly developed some improvisational skills that helped my scenes to feel a little more natural and fresh. This came in handy when I shot the scene where I speak to Denise in the Mercedes convertible. I worked on this scene a little more than the rest; it was a monologue and I had a lot of lines. I needed to be convincing and it was an important scene that would help the audience connect with my character. Michael and Berry knew how critical this scene was and they were hoping that I would pull it off. I nailed the scene and I improvised the line at the end, "Is it not kind of hot in here, Miss Charles?" During the recent 30th anniversary screenings, I really got to see how much people liked that scene and especially that line; audiences always laugh after I say it. It's a scene that really brings out Bruce Leroy's character and his unassuming nature. I think it's one of my best scenes in the film and Michael and Berry were really happy with it. It was also one of the scenes that helped to ease the tension that I had with Denise (she bit my neck during the rehearsal and left a serious hickey on me).

I enjoyed the fact that I was able to contribute to that scene, and I also creatively added to the film in other ways. I spoke to everyone on the film crew about how the Shaw Brothers movies always had a prologue before the action began, depicting the lead actor doing martial arts movements. I thought that was missing from *The Last Dragon* and I felt that it wouldn't be complete without it. The producers agreed with me, and they arranged for us to shoot a prologue scene after we had shot the rest of the film. They hired a director to work with me on the scene and I showed up to the set with a ton of ideas. I wanted to look just like Gordon Liu in all of those Shaw Brothers introductions, showing off my skills in front of an epic crimson background. However, when we actually shot the scene, we didn't get too complicated with it. I wanted to do a lot more, especially showing off some really cool and sophisticated stuff, but we chose to just do simple and really sharp-looking movements. It came out looking great, and I was pleased that my input made the film that much better.

I'm proud that people love this film so much, and I know that it has many special, iconic, fan favorite moments. Little kids always ask me about the thing in the tank in Eddie Arcadian's office. I used to tell them "You know, it wasn't a shark or a piranha, do you really think they would put the actor's life in danger by allowing me to put his head in a tank with some dangerous beast?" But I would never tell them what it was. It's a total secret. I like the fact that it's become a legendary mystery for people that have seen the movie! There are also some moments in the film that I'll never forget, though for different reasons. For example, there is a scene where I had a huge pimple that looked hilariously awful on the big screen. Hey, that's what happens when you make a movie when you're a teenager!

I really felt a strong personal connection to this movie. It was easy to imagine myself as Bruce Leroy, because we went to the same restaurants, walked on the same streets, and breathed the same air! The film was actually shot right in the neighborhoods I grew up in. The scene where Sho'nuff and his gang invade my parent's pizza shop was filmed on the lower east side of Manhattan somewhere around 12th or 13th Street. I used to live right around the corner from this location on 10th Street, and the place where I trained with Ron Van Clief was nearby as well. This whole neighborhood was my childhood stomping grounds and so it was truly like being at home.

When the filming was complete, I was caught up in the excitement and I was giddy with the idea that I was a real action hero. I didn't yet have the consciousness to think to myself, "Where do I go from here?" A working actor understands that you need to network, that you need the right agent, that you need the proper feedback and the ability to develop relationships with other creative professionals. I knew none of this since I came from the martial arts world, and my parents also couldn't guide me since they weren't actors themselves. Now that shooting had ended and the film was going to be released, I was about to learn some very important lessons about the entertainment world and how to survive in it.

Chapter 8 - Conflicts and Challenges

"Do not pray for an easy life, pray for the strength to endure a difficult one."

Bruce Lee

The post-production phase, where they add music and special effects, seemed to take forever. Post-production of a film usually takes longer than the actual shooting and can take several months to complete. It includes the complete editing of the picture, color correction on all of the edited scenes, and the addition of music. With *The Last Dragon*, Berry was making history in that he wanted the movie to have a music video vibe. There was music laid down in just about every scene of the movie and it was almost as much a musical as it was a martial arts adventure movie. After *The Last Dragon* was released, a lot of other films tried to capture this music video style. The movie was definitely ahead of its time.

At some point, the studio began to do test screenings so that they could see how people responded to the film. I got a call from Berry, who was at one of the screenings, and he said that the response to the film was "Extraordinary! People loved it! They were dancing in front of the screen during the end credits!" Berry handed the phone to someone else and it was Stevie Wonder. Obviously, he couldn't actually see the movie himself, but he must have had someone telling him what was going on in each scene. He told me how much he really loved the movie. I was impressed and flattered because I was such a huge fan of his.

There were some troubles with marketing, though. There was a power struggle between TriStar and Berry on how to market the picture. TriStar wanted to call the movie a "black film" and market it exclusively to African-American viewers. Berry, however, wanted the film to relate to everyone - black, white, young, old - and he felt that it would have a wide appeal. Unfortunately, TriStar ignored his advice and ultimately released *The Last Dragon* without any advertising to the white community. Even under these circumstances, the movie still enjoyed great success. The film even reached number two in box office sales in the country. I made the cover of many African-American teen magazines and the film was gaining a lot of popularity with African-American fans, but *The Last Dragon* just wasn't given the opportunity to find that wider audience that it deserved.

Back in the 80's, a film generally was able to get the top three box office spots if there were big stars in the movie. And even with a star-studded cast, a lot of money had to be spent on marketing, or the movie had to have extraordinary word-of-mouth. To stay near the top of the weekly box office sales, a film needs to be marketed to the vast American audience, black, white, and everyone in-between. A movie like Sylvester Stallone's *Rocky* didn't have many well-known faces, but the movie was a huge success due to the great story and the fact that it was marketed to everyone. *The Last Dragon* wasn't marketed to a wide audience and there weren't any big stars to help get the film any support from the mainstream press. Word-of-mouth about the film, however, was fantastic, and I truly believe that is what helped get the film the number two spot in the box office in 1985. But, eventually, it weathered away and left the theaters. We can only imagine what would have happened if it was marketed to more people.

However, the film gained a cult following, and I wasn't prepared for the sudden fame. A huge swarm of attention suddenly came my way but I was just a kid from New York City, trying to get my head together. There were many fun aspects to getting all that attention from everyone. I met many celebrities who came up to me and congratulated me. When I went to the premiere in Los Angeles, it was like going to the Oscars! I met so many famous actors and big names, like Ernest Borgnine and one of my childhood crushes, Cheryl Ladd from *Charlie's Angels*. Cheryl actually came over to me and hugged me, telling me how great I was. It was a surreal and magical moment. I didn't know how to navigate through all of this newfound attention. I needed professional guidance, whether from a manager or a therapist (or probably both).

Eventually, there was a contract negotiation about doing sequels to *The Last Dragon* and maybe some other films for Motown. This was an exciting idea to me. The film was loved by a lot of people but didn't get the exposure it really could have had for me as an actor. I thought that the sequels would be wonderful and even more successful, and I was sure that Berry would make me a bigger star. We had become great friends and I really saw him as my mentor. I stayed at his house in Beverly Hills, and he took me to some interesting places, including the Playboy Mansion. Berry even took me to a family birthday party for one of his grandsons, who is now known as Redfoo, one of the lead singers for the colorful pop group LMFAO. They actually gave Bruce Leroy a shout out in their 2011 smash hit "Sexy and I Know It". I really believed I had a strong relationship with Berry and that we were going to work together to make many more great films.

I was asked to have a contract meeting with Berry and Suzanne De Passe, who was on the business side of things, and I was really looking forward to it. I learned the hard way that Berry wasn't quite the friend I thought he was. When my attorney and I landed in Los Angeles and walked into the meeting at Motown Headquarters, we were walking into a lion's den. Unexpectedly, Berry was not present at the meeting, but only Suzanne was there. I immediately noticed that the atmosphere was extremely tense. Suzanne was never super friendly towards me, but she was especially rough on that day. When my lawyer and I began discussing the contract, Suzanne reacted very defensively. She continuously insulted my abilities, saying things like, "You're not really that talented, Taimak," and "You're not that great after all." My attorney didn't pay attention to her antics but I took it to heart. I was a sensitive kid and I didn't understand the mind games that Suzanne and Berry were playing. I had thought we were all a family. Now that Suzanne was being so cold and rude, I was confused and disoriented.

I didn't realize it back then, but this is actually a typical entertainment business strategy: the good cop and the bad cop. It's a way for producers to manipulate the artist so that they can get what they want. Basically, the good cop behaves like your friend and gets you to open up to him, so that you let him know your concerns, your insecurities, and skills you think you might lack. He gets you to tell him the sort of things that you wouldn't want to share during contract negotiations. But the good cop brings this information to the bad cop, so that they can use it against you and not budge an inch during the negotiations.

After speaking with Suzanne, my attorney pulled me into another room and told me that he thought it wasn't a good contract and that I shouldn't sign it. He felt that we could negotiate a better deal that wasn't so exploitative, and he was convinced that they would be willing to give me a higher upfront salary or points on the film (having points on the film means that I could take a lower upfront salary but make a percentage of the film's profits). At the time, I probably would have signed just about anything. I knew that there weren't many actors who had the opportunity to star in a successful movie series, especially if they were men of color. I also really trusted Berry. If he had been there and explained things to me, I would have gone for it, even if the deal wasn't perfect. I felt like it was his responsibility as mentor to sit me down and go over the contract with me, sharing his insights and helping me understand how the deal would be good for me in the long run. But he wasn't there and I felt alone. I followed my attorney's advice and didn't sign the contract.

After that day, I never heard from Berry again. He didn't return my calls. I was just a kid and he was my mentor, and I would have done anything that he asked of me. He had been so close to me during the making of the film and then he dropped me completely when he didn't need me any longer. I briefly ran into him a few months later and he was very uptight and aloof. That's when I knew it was really over and I couldn't count on him. It was a very lonely, frustrating feeling for me, while at the same time it was a very eye-opening experience.

I later heard that people were saying I didn't sign because of my ego; sure, I had an ego, just like everyone in Hollywood did, but that was far from the truth. It's complicated, but I'll explain why things didn't work out in a little more detail, and I hope you young talented artists out there are paying close attention. I believe that what you believe about yourself is reflected in how you present yourself to other people. When you take a moment to do some introspection and be completely open and honest with yourself, you will find that you have underlying insecurities that have seeped into your way of being. When these insecurities aren't seriously addressed and confronted, there are discrepancies between who you believe you are on the inside, and how you portray yourself on the outside. And this is exactly what was going on with me at the time. Until I truly understood myself in a way that I could honestly acknowledge and recognize my special and unique qualities, I wasn't going to be able to understand how I was presenting myself to others.

After I paid my taxes, I had roughly $15,000 from *The Last Dragon*, which was spent in just a few months. I bought a car and new clothes, and I went out with friends, having a good time. I never learned about finance or how to capitalize on the success I just had. "You're as good as your last picture," they say. Well...that was my last picture. The years went by quickly.

During these years, I met a few people that were upfront and helpful but I also met a whole bunch of opportunists and dishonest folks. I hadn't developed good radar for these phonies. For instance, I was eventually able to get a meeting with a huge agent at one the top agencies in the world, and I was excited about it. The agent appeared so helpful and genuinely interested in collaborating with me to develop and expand my career. When I left, he shook my hand and even gave me a hug. However, he never returned my calls after that meeting. This agent promised the world and delivered nothing. On top of that guy being a flake, he was later busted for raping a young lady who was one of his clients. Unfortunately, he was just one in a long line of flakey people who I would encounter in the entertainment industry.

My optimism diminished with every year that passed and every job that wasn't booked. I was eating oatmeal and noodles and just trying to get by. I was only getting small jobs here and there. One job I booked was a Coke commercial featuring the New Kids on the Block. We shot on the beach, mostly with a bunch of models and NKOTB. It was actually really fun, jumping around and goofing in the sun. I also worked at Universal Studios for about a year as part of the *Miami Vice* stunt show. So I was able to get by, but I wasn't always doing the most fun or prestigious projects.

I finally booked a starring gig in a film called *The White Girl*, opposite the actress Troy Byer. Tony Brown, the producer of the film, was known for his PBS talk show, *Tony Brown's Journal*. He discussed everything from AIDS to black politics and many other issues. It was a serious talk show about important issues. He wrote, produced and directed *The White Girl*, and he had a very specific vision about how to market the film. He planned to go to each city, rent theaters to play the film, and extensively market it to the African-American communities in that city. He wanted to take this concept on the road and travel across all of America. It wasn't a bad idea, but during those times with no social media or the internet being part of the daily culture, it was much more difficult. It would have been an even better concept if the film was good, but it wasn't.

Some of the situations in the film were just too outlandish to appeal to a wide-ranging audience. I periodically pointed these out to Tony Brown, but he wasn't really open to anyone's suggestions. The two other leads - Troy Byer and a good actor named O.L. Duke, who played the bad guy - also felt a bit uncomfortable with some of the ideas. But when an actor is getting his or her paycheck, a lot of times they just go through the motions and follow the director's choices. It's understandable, of course. Who wants to wait tables or eat oatmeal every day? So why rock the boat? It's better to just zip it, especially when the director isn't open to suggestions. Most of our suggestions were primarily about how to update the style of the film. For example, O.L. Duke wore a white cape, like some clown from a 1970's black exploitation movie. O.L. and I joked about it, but he knew he had to wear it so he just toughed it out. He was so cool...we became good friends. Unfortunately, he passed away in a car crash a few years back. I miss him.

That was my first serious role after *The Last Dragon* and I don't think I was very good in the movie. I wasn't confident in my technique as an actor and I also wasn't that confident in the material or the director.

When those things happen, the actor has to rely on his or her own resources to pull out a worthy performance. I just didn't have enough knowledge and experience to pull from. But for better or worse, *The White Girl* was completed and released. The movie didn't do too well, but there were some folks who enjoyed it. Personally, I didn't like it. I just felt that it was too cheesy. There were a couple of funny moments and a few nice interactions between Troy and myself, but overall, I believe that Tony Brown's style was dated. I know that sounds blunt, but I just want to be honest and that's the way I felt. However, I do commend him on finishing the film and going all out to have a vision on how to market an African-American movie.

I still get twisted in my head, when I find myself falling into the trap of saying that a movie is a "black" movie or a "white" movie. Our society is so backwards that we have to label films or that we even think in those terms. I do understand, of course. I know that we all have our differences, but there are more similarities than differences and I'm happy to say that I see things changing. However, it's still tough to get a sophisticated movie made that stars people of color in the lead roles. The entertainment industry keeps things as conservative as possible. The message sent to Hollywood screenwriters is, "Hey, make sure to make it a black movie, and make sure that you add those cliché characters in your script. You know, the funny black guy, or the big black tough guy, or the loud, fat black girl." Yes I know they do exist, but you can also find people like that in many different races and from many different cultural backgrounds. Unfortunately, the message is that if you don't follow the rules and stick to the stereotypes, we're going to pass on your script. When a script is laid down on a table at a studio they shouldn't have to label it as a black film. It would be much better if they just called it a great script on its own terms and they could go about finding an excellent, diverse cast for it.

In the past few decades, people have tried to speak up about this problem in the movie business. For instance, organizations like the NAACP were extremely critical of Hollywood's black exploitation films from the 70's and they had a fair argument. The NAACP complained that the roles that were given to black men were stereotypical and didn't garner any dignity, which was true. The roles on TV were the same, with positive roles few and far between. In the 80's, there was an even bigger dry spell when it came to men of color in film. Hollywood simply wasn't shooting films with leading men of color and I had no idea how to build a career for myself as a "black man". Denzel Washington was starting to come up and he had a lot of success. His career brought optimism to men of color, but we almost felt like he was the exception to the rule. I couldn't wait around for the industry to change. I had to pay rent and I needed to eat. I was overwhelmed by the whole thing. At the time, there just wasn't work out there for someone that looked like me.

Of course, in the end, this industry is a business. It's all about what will be the most successful and profitable. The production companies are only willing to take a chance on an image that will sell. If I wasn't going to be "black" in the way that they wanted, I wasn't going to get any roles or opportunities. It's a shame, because there are so many talented artists out there who are willing to pour out their heart and soul on the screen, the stage, or the canvas, but money and the conservative nature of popular culture holds them back. I was one of those artists, working hard and prepared to lay all of my emotions on the line, but I just wasn't given the proper chance to do it. I was slowly starting to understand the way that the business worked, but I still had to go through a lot of hard lessons. I knew that things weren't going to get easier anytime soon...but I couldn't give up.

A Scene from *The Professor*

The Professor is an action/thriller screenplay about a philosophy professor named Frank who has a dark past. He thinks that he has left his path behind him, but he tries to help a student and gets sucked back into a world of crime and violence. In this scene, Frank asks his students if they are able to recognize the most important and foundational of all philosophical questions. He is interrupted by Tony, a student that has constantly been disruptive in the class...

INT. CALVIN SINGER UNIVERSITY- CLASSROOM- DAY

Frank goes back to what he was speaking about before his lecture was interrupted by TONY. Tony is 20, white, independent, edgy, spoiled. He looks anxious, eager, ruthless.

TONY

Psychology.

Frank pauses again and calmly looks at Tony. Tony's giving him a smile. Frank continues, not flustered by Tony's interruption.

FRANK

Absolutism.

TONY (stern)

Is it related to psychology? Answer my question.

Frank pauses for a moment, waiting for his next move.

FRANK

Yes, it is related to psychology, as I was explaining. Egoism, Absolutism, Intuitionism, etc. are associated with mental and behavioral patterns.

Frank will elaborate further about how some of these ideas are related to psychology, while we pan around the classroom. Tony looks over to Lance and smiles. Lance is 19, AFRICAN AMERICAN, he shakes his head in disbelief.

Frank goes back to what he talked about before Tony interrupted.

FRANK (CONT'D)

As I was saying we want to discuss a few of those conceptual frameworks. ABSOLUTISM, EGOISM, etc. Does someone else care to tread into these waters and offer your opinion?

LANCE

It's a known fact that God knows all. He knows the moment that each of us would be born, how we would live our lives, when each of us will die, and whether or not we're going to heaven or hell.

CARMEN, another student, rolls her eyes.

PETER SEIBERT asks Professor Carter a question. Peter is 20, white, from a middle class family, overall a good kid.

PETER

What are the dates for these?

FRANK

November 10th. However, all of this information can be found on your syllabus and I sent an e-mail to everyone that registered for the class a week ago. Check your e-mail.

PROFESSOR CARTER finishes the class and dismisses everyone. All the students head out as we see the FRAT BROS - Tony, Lance, Jonathan, Peter and a few others - talking.

TONY (to Peter)

Don't forget 'bout the party.

PETER

You're kidding right?

TONY

Connor's gonna kill him.

Tony kicks Jonathan, and they begin to roughhouse each other. All of them start to fight with each other in a playful way. They're just goofing off.

JONATHAN

Not too sure 'bout this one.

Jonathan goes to take Tony down with a wrestling move.

Frank watches them. CLOSE UP on Frank as he goes into a trance-like state. A drop of sweat falls from his temple.

Next thing you know he's right on top of the boys, he strikes them without causing any serious damage. His moves are fast and impressive. He does a combination of martial arts strikes on them and he sweeps Tony's feet out from under him. Before you can blink an eye, he's directly above Tony, holding him down as if ready to strike him.

Tony and the rest of the boys are surprised to say the least. Frank realizes what he's done and snaps out of it. The boys' jaws are dropped to the floor, mesmerized by the moves they just saw.

FRANK

Hey guys, uhm, don't play around like
that. Get going, huh..okay?

The boys stay silent for a couple of seconds, and then...

PETER

Dude! Wow, where you learn how to do that?

LANCE

Holy shit! Did you see that?

TONY (pissed but still shocked)

Kinda shocking, teach.

FRANK

Get going guys. See you tomorrow.

TONY

Ahh, yeah.

The boys leave. They seem to love what they saw, but Frank was anxious that they might let someone know, which would put his job on the line. Frank gets his books together, grabs his bag, and bolts out.

Chapter 9 – Surviving in the Industry

"Think lightly of yourself and deeply of the world."

Miyamoto Musashi

In the years after *The Last Dragon*, I had a lot of growing to do, and I needed to learn a lot about myself. I had to learn the game of life and I had to find the master within me. I was looking for stardom and the big payday like everyone else, but I was starting to realize that just getting a big movie role wasn't the answer.

In 1987, a good friend of my mom's passed away. His name was William Donnell Smith, known to his friends as Willie, and he was considered to be one of the most successful young African-American designers in the fashion industry. His sister, Tookie, was dating Robert De Niro, and I met them both at Willie's wake. The wake had a very somber and contemplative atmosphere, so we didn't get to speak much, but a number of people told De Niro about me and how great I was in *The Last Dragon*. De Niro was interested in meeting me, and we were eventually able to meet and get to know each other a bit. He introduced me to his son, Raphael, and asked me if I would mentor Raphael and teach him martial arts.

Raphael was a cute kid, about 10 years-old. I wound up becoming Raphael's sensei, but I was really more like his big brother. I taught him twice a week, on and off, for about a year, and a lot of the time we would just bond. We had a great relationship, and his family was very happy that he liked seeing me. I even took him out to the Six Flags Great Adventure theme park with a bunch of my friends, and we all had a blast. When Raphael got his martial arts basics down, I took him to the Bronx to spar with some kids there. One kid was bigger than Raphael and he was pretty nervous. Even though he was scared, he toughened up and gave it his best, and he did better than I thought he would!

De Niro was really cool and down to earth, and he was a good friend to me. He did his best to help me out with my career and he even set me up with a huge casting director, Bonnie Timmerman. What I really needed, though, was a professional business manager who would be able to work with me full-time. I also needed a good therapist and a spiritual advisor - people who would be able to guide me through the issues and emotional obstacles that I was facing. I was only 22 at the time and I needed some real guidance so that I could navigate these complicated waters and take advantage of my talents.

Around that time, I was introduced to an interesting guy named George Tan. Tan was a huge fan of *The Last Dragon* and a native New Yorker, and he had worked on traditional martial arts films in China. Tan was young and ambitious, and he wanted to make a great martial arts movie with me. I continued to meet with Tan and we gradually worked out what this potential movie was going to be. Before long, *The Black Ninja* took shape, and I was excited about the idea of getting in front of the camera again in a starring role.

We began shooting *The Black Ninja* in the Bronx, and I had many of my martial artist friends come out, such as Nathan Ingram, Jerry "Fast Feet" Fontanez and his student Fabian Carrillo, and others. We were all very young and excited to be a part of the film. The project was on a shoestring budget...we didn't have any of the modern conveniences like digital movie cameras that would let you capture amazing quality video for a fraction of the price of real film, and almost all of the production's money went into the actual film that we were shooting on. When your budget was only $100,000 to $200,000 and you were shooting on film, every cent goes to buying the film and editing it the old way. It was expensive! Nowadays, of course, almost any creative kid can put together some digital equipment and come up with a great little movie, but back then was a very different time for cheap, independent-style filmmaking.

Unfortunately, *The Black Ninja* didn't work out and we didn't finish shooting. It wasn't for a lack of trying. The film was a lofty and ambitious attempt at capitalizing on *The Last Dragon*'s popularity but they ran out of money and only shot a few scenes, mostly some short fight sequences. I couldn't complain too much; it wasn't like Hollywood was looking for more roles for me. You would think that there would be plenty of producers trying to get me in their projects, but Hollywood doesn't work that way. Even though I was the lead in a successful film, I wasn't white or Hollywood Black. In other words, I didn't fit into one of the stereotypical roles that Hollywood likes for black men to take - funny or ghetto. It also didn't help that I didn't have a reputable agent or manager for a while after I got out of the contract with Berry.

I went back and forth between New York and Los Angeles, trying to get parts and just making ends meet. One day, I got a call from Bethann Hardison, an agent from a modeling agency. She said that Janet Jackson wanted me to play her boyfriend in a new music video from her *Control* album. The song was called "Let's Wait Awhile" and it was going be directed by Dominic Sena. I asked the production company what I would be paid for the video, and it was laughable - $500! I didn't know it at the time, but companies almost always low ball you at first, hoping you'll be excited you got a job and just take it. I knew Janet was a big name and rising to the top, so I knew I should get a lot more. I got Bethann on the phone and I told her, "Sorry, but I can't do it for that fee." I told her the fee I wanted - $3500 – and it was approved right away. We started shooting the following week, and it was an exciting opportunity for me. I always knew that I would have great on-screen chemistry with Janet and now I would get the chance to prove it.

When we started shooting, it was the middle of winter and very cold, around 10 degrees. They fitted me in some warm clothes and then Janet arrived with her boyfriend. She was never alone and he was always with her during rehearsals, meals, etc. He was a bit of a Svengali. Even when we would be shooting, he was always really close to the camera, like he was directing the video. I thought the director Dominic Sena was really patient and professional about the whole thing. Janet also had three big bodyguards who looked like they belonged on *The Sopranos*. They were off-duty cops who worked with Janet whenever she came to town, and they were real wisecrackers. They would goof on her boyfriend a lot and try to make me laugh, saying things like "Hey Taimak, when you do that scene with her, tell her you want her right now and that you don't want to wait awhile." I just laughed – I sure wasn't trying to start anything with Janet. I'm not a home wrecker and who is to say she wanted anyone other than her boyfriend at the time. The rest of the video went smoothly and it turned out really well. People always tell me how much they loved it, and it was definitely a highlight of my early career after *The Last Dragon*.

After shooting that video, I did a lot of other different gigs and had a lot of different projects going on. I wasn't always going in the direction that I wanted, but I was getting small opportunities here and there. For instance, I was hired to model in a workshop for the VH1 Awards. I had a great time and we all did some really interesting work. It was especially interesting because Ben Stiller was there, working on ideas for his Zoolander character. Stiller was awesome to work with. He was intelligent, unique, and very humble. When I went to the theater to see the final version of his character in the *Zoolander* film, I rooted for it to be a success. It definitely was, and the rest is history – it made Stiller into an even bigger star.

I even tried my hand at doing stand-up comedy and I did a few spots at The Comedy Store on Sunset Boulevard in West Hollywood. It was a really interesting scene, because there were so many young comics who were hungry and eager to achieve success. When all of these comics were together, you could sense their anxiety and intensity. They were ready to take the industry by storm as soon as someone gave them a chance. Some of these comics broke through and got their chance and some didn't. I met Eddie Griffin there and he told me that he was a fan of *The Last Dragon*. He would always crack me up when I saw him and I thought he was a really likable guy. He was dirt broke at the time and once in a while I would give him a ride home. I was really happy for him when he developed a TV show called *The Malcolm and Eddie Show*, which he created with Malcolm Jamal Warner of *The Cosby Show* fame. I appeared on the show as a guest star, which was a lot of fun.

Back then, being in the Hollywood scene meant running around with a lot of wild and unique people. I met up with Eddie Murphy a bunch of times; I heard he really liked *The Last Dragon*, and he even rented out a theater in New Jersey to watch it with his homeboys. Eddie eventually contacted me and we took a drive to watch the new release of one of his films, *Beverly Hills Cop ll*. He liked to drive around the block outside of a theater and get a feel for how long the line was so that he could judge whether or not it would be a success. In this case, it definitely was! It was the mid 80's and Eddie was one of the biggest celebrities in the country. Swarms of fans were always showing up wherever he went - it was a memorable time.

Eddie actually had an impact on my career a few years before this. After *The Last Dragon* came out and the contract deal fell through with Berry Gordy and Motown, my father thought it would be a good idea for me to get a top manager. Eddie Murphy's manager had an office nearby on the east side of Manhattan, and my father felt that he would be the perfect man for the job. My father set up an appointment for us and it seemed like it would be a great opportunity. The manager was pretty nice and thought that he could do something for me and my career. Unfortunately, he called us later that week and told us that Eddie Murphy didn't want him to manage me. The deal was killed. Eddie was a huge star at the time and his manager did not want to challenge him on this. I'm not sure why Eddie was against this. Maybe he felt that his manager's time was already stretched thin.

Whatever his reasons at the time, Eddie eventually saw me as a colleague and friend. He introduced me to his other friends like Rick James, Keenen Ivory Wayans, and the rest of his crew. Rick James was nothing but laughs. He was loud and obnoxious, but had a special charisma to go with it. You either loved him or hated him, and he didn't really care. Whenever I saw him since we met, no matter where we were or how public the setting was, he would scream my name at the top of his lungs, "Taimak! Come over here, nigga!!" If he was with a lady, he would turn to her and shout, "Bitch, do you know who this nigga is?! He's the motherfuckin' *last dragon*!" Rick just had a special way of acknowledging you, and he always had me in stitches.

Despite meeting a lot of people during the years after *The Last Dragon*, it was rare to really make a lasting connection with anyone. When I did, it was something I really held onto and cherish. I formed a nice friendship with Mike Tyson and we were mutual fans. One Saturday night, Mike called me up and said, "Tai, what are you doing? I want you to come down to The Tunnel and meet somebody." The Tunnel was a popular nightclub in Manhattan, and I met Mike at the club's bar about an hour later. I could tell from his voice on the phone that he was excited about something, and I kind of figured that it must be about a girl.

Mike Tyson and I visiting Ron Van Clief on the lower east side of Manhattan.

Sure enough, Mike introduced me to his new girlfriend, the actress Robin Givens. He was completely smitten with her and passionate about their new relationship. My first impression was not very positive. Based on their chemistry together, I had a gut feeling that this was not the girl for him. I didn't know how to communicate to him that I didn't think this would work out. I mean, how could I be of any help with his relationship, though? I was having my own problems, and my own relationships with women weren't exactly working out. After Mike got married to Givens everything went downhill for him, especially the difficult to watch Barbara Walters interview. I never heard from him much after he got married. We've only seen each other twice in the past 30 years, and he was warm the first time but very distant the next.

I felt like I needed a change, so I went to live in Miami. I needed some sunshine, in every sense of the word. I worked with Irene Marie Models in South Beach. I ran on the beach a lot and continued my martial arts training, staying in top shape. I really enjoyed training in the sun on the sand. After a few weeks in Miami, I was lucky enough to book a big commercial. They told us the casting would be on the beach and for the women to wear bikinis and the men to wear boxer shorts. There were about thirty girls when I got there and about the same number of guys. They had a video camera set up on a tripod in the sand and they gave us simple directions. They said, "Take a number and when we call your number, state your name and height and then turn around slowly." We each took our turn and left. The next day, I was told I got the job, and I was super excited.

It turned out to be a really high-paying commercial. I made about $67,000 because it played during the Super Bowl.

One day, my modeling agent called and told me that Gianni Versace was casting for his new ad line, and that I should be at the agency to meet with him that afternoon. When I arrived, there was a whole bunch of people lined up to meet with Mr. Versace so that he could look at our book of photos. I had just printed some pictures for my portfolio, including some edgy pictures featuring partial nudity. When Versace called me over, he greeted me and started skimming through my book, then paused at one of the edgy photos. He must have stared at it for a good ten seconds. It was kind of awkward because he never said anything and he just looked at the picture the whole time.

It was definitely a great picture. I remember when we shot that photo: it was really early in the morning and you couldn't see much because it was so foggy on the beach. The photographer kept shooting away while a friend and I tumbled around on the sand, having a ball, just running around like a bunch of monkeys and acting crazy. At some point, I did a handstand while opening my legs into a split, and my friend said to hold that position. He ran full speed towards me and did a front somersault over my legs, and the photographer captured the shot. It came out really well!

Versace closed my book and said thank you, and then I left. Unfortunately, I didn't book the job. In the entertainment business, you get used to it and you know that you can't get every job. But a couple of days later I looked at my portfolio and noticed that my great picture was gone! I was a bit pissed that my picture was taken without my consent and without me getting the job. I was also upset because, out of the many models that were chosen, there wasn't a single person of color in any of the shots. A lot of black models and talent didn't stay in Miami very long, because they knew that it would be difficult for them to get jobs. I decided to leave Miami. I knew that Los Angeles and New York had their own problems, but I was still able to get steady work in those cities.

I kept working my way through the industry and tried not to be dismayed. I saw plenty of other martial arts actors getting work, like Jean-Claude Van Damme and Steven Seagal. I didn't see why I couldn't get some of those same roles. I certainly recognized their talent - they each had a distinct, unique aspect to them - but I also knew that I could be just as great. I felt like everyone else was passing me by on the way to the top. When I was in New York, I became friends with Vin Diesel before he got his big break. When Vin came out to Los Angeles, I helped him to find a good place to do Brazilian Jiu-Jitsu. I only saw him a few times after that, though. I also met with Wesley Snipes many times, and he was a fan of both my martial arts ability and my work in *The Last Dragon*. He always tried to see if he could find something for me in his *Blade* series, but he never found me a part. He knew I was talented and he believed in me, but he didn't think the available roles were strong enough for me. That was okay, of course. Those films were his thing and I had to find my way.

It's difficult to find your own way, though. Sometimes, you need to make some really tough choices. For instance, I had a meeting with the company that was producing the *American Ninja* films. In those movies, Michael Dudikoff was the hero, and his sidekick was played by an actor named Steve James. Steve James was an African-American martial artist from New York, and I really enjoyed and admired his work. Unfortunately, Steve died in 1993, which was tough to hear. When Steve died, the *American Ninja* producers were looking for another African-American martial artist to take over his role, and they were interested in me.

Unfortunately, they wanted to shoot the next film in apartheid South Africa. Many entertainers were willing to go to South Africa. The government was paying a lot of money to attract film productions and it was very tempting. However, the country's race relations were deeply troubling and they had a horrible reputation for civil rights abuses. I chose to pass on the project after the meeting, even though I really needed the money and was excited about the opportunity. There comes a point where you need to stand up for your values and stick to what you believe in. I could have taken the *American Ninja* job and made some good money and gotten nice exposure, but I would have been participating in something that went against what was important to me as a person.

Today, it feels so good to be older and wiser, not making the same mistakes over and over. When I was younger, though, I was stuck in my own head. I felt I wasn't living up to my potential, and there was so much more that I wanted to do. I needed to find a new way to express myself. If I wanted to live and survive in this industry, I would have to change the entire way that I approached the idea of performance. I decided that it was time for me to really dive into the art and craft of serious acting.

Weather the Storm

Shadows follow me day and night, is the clock
backing up or moving ahead?

Imposing my will on unshakable ground, it seems

Looking out for love not lust but the sweat and taste
of it pulls me in

I want to fill my soul with silence, posing questions
to the unquestionable

Is an ongoing link to a progressive action or to be
more clear just a waste of time

Time is endless in your hands, my lord, is it endless
in mine too

There I go again posing that unquestionable question

Leaps and bounds existing within me all to be
enlisted to perform

Outside of me a contract, a bet, an arrangement

With myself to find myself now, not tomorrow or
yesterday, *c'est la vie*

I said to myself the other day if love feels good stick around and

Enjoy the benefits employed by the ultimate

And ahh, the pulse of love when it ceases to exist just falls away like

An unsolvable puzzle, let it go, be uncertain for a little while and recover sanity

But when it's all good treat it good, take small and large

Quantities at different times or all at once

That unshakable love that unquestionable question marriage

To be or not to be

Have the courage or at least act as though you do, maybe you will find yourself

I'm a stranger in this lonely land with dreams of a faraway place

I know it exists with only a bridge of life lessons to cross holding onto his key

I sit back and watch myself licking my wounds and I get back on

The material road in the material world

But I'm a part of that machine I exist because of it
and it because of me

And that faraway place I spoke of, that utopia of bliss

An iridescent drop and the vast land of performers
waiting for an Oscar

The Olympics, The Goodwill Hunting Games

Then I say peace be unto you your souls and may all
your faithful dreams

Be met with a smile and a kiss

Be healthy

Super excited. I got my first suit, Tom & Jerry shirt, my father's custom-made lahme belt and Converse sneakers, 1975.

Sad day. My first day of school at 4 years old, 1969. Photograph by my teacher.

The Hayes family, 1957

Family shot of me (on the right), my father, my mother, my sister Naria and my brother Meishan

Taimak Guarriello

My high school yearbook picture, Brandies High School 1982

Posing with Joe (cutman) after a kickboxing fight in NY, 1984

Posing with fellow Ron Van Clief students. I was 16 and ready for war. Photo by Glen Perry.

Julius J. Carry III (aka Sho'nuff) drooling down my neck during our last fight scene in "The Last Dragon". Picture courtesy of Sony Pictures

Denise Matthews (Vanity) and I at the premier of "The Last Dragon".

Cover of Inside Karate after "The Last Dragon" was released.

OKMAG Winter '85 Cover of Official Karate Magazine
Photo Courtesy of Official Karate Magazine™

On Break with Janet Jackson and security et al, 1987

My childhood crush Donyale Luna, the first Black super model.

Summer 1985 Black Belt Yearbook. Costume by Sir William,
for kids martial arts show, Masters – 1995
Photo courtesy of Wright's Media

One of the sweet scenes with Denise Matthews (Vanity)
Photo courtesy of Sony Entertainment

Shaolin Kung Fu certificate of excellence. Sifu Shi Yang Ming, 2003

Flyer for Off-Broadway show, *Roadhouse the Comedy*, 2004

Leo and I in the Harlem, NY Hospital after he was shot, 2011.

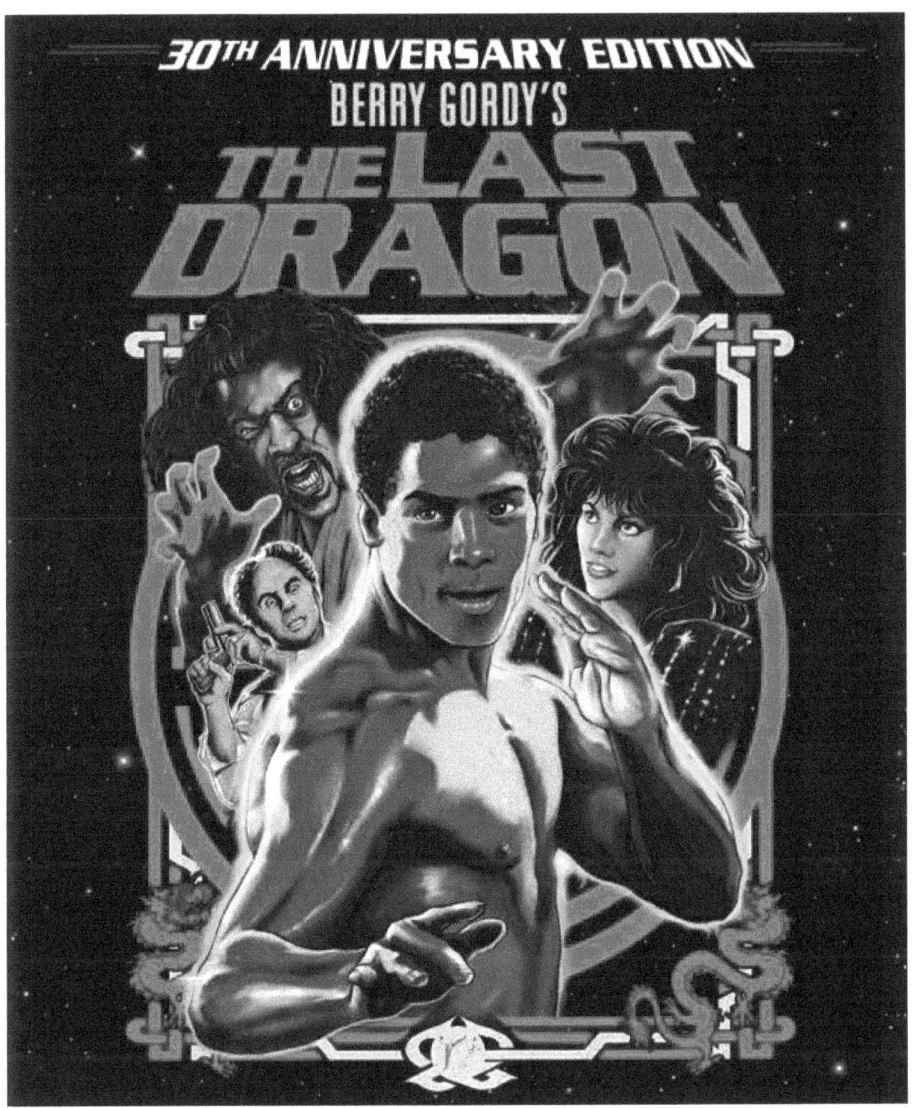

30th anniversary Blu Ray cover by acclaimed Mondo artist
Gary Pullin.
Berry Gordy's *The Last Dragon* now available on Blu-ray™
Image courtesy of Sony Entertainment.

Posing with my new fan, Elijah Wood during the 30th anniversary screening at the Drafthouse in Austin, TX, 2015

My two five-year-old nieces, Skyla and Gianna with my mother in the background.

Jim Kelly and I at one of the comic conventions. He was a true
gentleman and one of my heroes.
Photo by Rene Carson, HIT PICTURES

My dad gave me this photo. Looking up at the eagle –
Taimak, Striking Eagle.

Chapter 10 - Lessons in Life and Acting

"Without wonder and insight, acting is just a business. With it, it becomes creation."

Bette Davis

When I was dating Carla Brothers, she really opened up my eyes to the idea of acting as a creative craft. I took many acting classes and I worked on many different scenes with different acting partners. I read a lot of books about acting and learned to develop a character. The discipline of developing the craft felt very organic and natural to me. It was very similar to building the foundation of a house. I loved it and I truly felt that I was cultivating something beautiful.

I attended scene study and technique classes at HB Studios in the West Village. The studio is still there at 120 Bank Street, in a nice, quiet part of the Village. When you walked through the door of the studio, the atmosphere was very friendly and cozy, and the entire place gave off a warm and comfortable feeling. It was in one of those old brownstone buildings which made you feel like you're a part of New York history. At the classes, I mostly worked with Earle Hyman, who played Dr. Huxtable's dad on *The Cosby Show*; he was an older gentleman (he was already in his 80's when we started working together) and he was a very kind and helpful mentor.

Working with Earle and great actors from other schools like William Esper Studio, really helped me improve my acting skills. I was able to grow as an actor because I was open-minded and receptive to all of their advice and recommendations. Sometimes it wasn't even about what the actors and teachers told me…it was just that they were there, and I vibed off of their energy.

I eventually learned that the key to great acting is to be in tune with the people around you. I believe that the ability to connect is truly imperative if you want to be a great actor. I didn't understand that when I was younger, but I definitely get it now. I read a book about the legendary film director, Elia Kazan. He said that working in the acting business has less to do with talent and more to do with how to work in a community environment. I never forgot that and it has really stuck with me. If you want to be a successful actor, you need to be open to the people you work with and embrace the community aspect of performance. I really wanted to become a good actor and I knew I could do it. The more I developed as a man, the better my acting became. Despite my improvements though, I wasn't great at the audition process. I couldn't memorize lines as well as some actors. When I had an audition the next day and there was a lot of text to memorize, I didn't have the confidence that I could learn everything in time and pull the audition off. Auditioning isn't about memorizing lines, it's really about understanding your role and giving a good performance, but it really freed me up when I did know the lines well.

I did end up landing a few big commercials, and that kept me solid for quite a while. I still couldn't get any film roles, though. It was a rough feeling. I never told my parents about the struggles that I was going through. I always put my best face on when I saw them and said, "Everything is great." I knew a lot of other actors who were getting parts here and there, but sometimes they had to go out and create roles for themselves. For instance, my friend Fabian was a prosperous insurance salesman in Los Angeles, but he was really interested in becoming a movie star. He was getting his feet wet in Hollywood and trying to find his way, earning his living with insurance while hustling to join in on any film or TV production that he could. Fabian was ultimately able to use his persistence and business knowledge to make his own movie, *The Latin Dragon*, and I was extremely proud of him. I started to wonder if that was also the path for me…would I have to take the initiative and make my own opportunities? Would I have to create my own roles?

One day, a cinematographer recognized me at a café. He came over and said, "Taimak! I'm getting together a little film and it's being financed by these two brothers who have some money. I'd love to know if you're interested in playing a role. It's definitely a low budget film, but we'll pay you." I met with him again and read the script. It was a corny story but they would pay me $20,000 for the part. Who doesn't want $20,000, right? I needed the money, and I wanted to help out my family as much as I could. I would also get to play the lead bad guy – a sinister con artist with a group of followers – and it was a chance to take on a different kind of role.

I was studying Method acting at the time. Method acting is an acting technique developed by a Russian theater director named Constantin Stanislavski, made popular by Lee Strasburg and Uta Hagen after many famous actors studied with them, including Marlon Brando, Marilyn Monroe, and Paul Newman, to name a few. The Method, as it is known, teaches actors to "become the character," so you have to really jump into your role and truly inhabit the character. Sometimes, a Method actor will stay in character even when he isn't shooting the movie - he needs to convince himself that he really *is* the character he is playing.

In this film, I was going to play a real asshole, a horrible gangster. I embraced the role and imagined that I really *was* this horrible gangster! One of the other actors told me, "Taimak, do whatever you want with me, I'm a Method actor too. Don't worry about being nice to me." He was playing one of my minions in the gang and my character was supposed to be awful and abusive to him. He should have never given me that permission. I wanted to inhabit my character and really live up to the part, so I treated this actor like crap. I would say things to him like, "Hey knucklehead, go get a shave. You look like shit." I took this Method acting stuff too literally and I said a lot of other mean things. I didn't do or say anything that was *too* outrageous, but I was pretty rude and nasty to him.

One morning, while we were getting ready to shoot a scene, this actor didn't report to the set. We couldn't find him anywhere and we couldn't start shooting without him. We looked for him but no one knew where he was. I finally got a knock on my door and everyone asked, "Taimak, what did you do to him?" I was shocked and I wasn't sure what they were talking about. This actor had apparently been found sleeping in his car, slumped over the steering wheel. He had gone out and gotten wasted the night before, and had even defecated on himself. Many of the cast members blamed me and I definitely felt horrible about it. I didn't think it was my fault, though. He was a grown man, and I felt like he should have known that this was all part of the Method performance. At the same time, I hope that he has forgiven me.

I ultimately found out that this production hadn't completed their Screen Actors Guild union requirements. This put me in jeopardy with the union and I couldn't continue doing the film. The producers tried to get me to stick around so they could finish shooting. But they weren't honest with me and they tried to keep me in the dark about everything. This wasn't a joke, though – I could have gotten kicked out of the union and that would have jeopardized all of my acting work for years to come. Although I wanted to finish making the film, I was forced to walk away while we were halfway through shooting. It's not my voice in the whole movie. They ended up using a white guys voice, because they lost some sound on the film, it was a mess.

I wanted to find acting roles that were more prestigious and that really challenged me as a performer. In order to do that, I had to find an acting community that took the craft seriously. I decided to find a new school that would help me to develop as an actor. I found what I was looking for at the Beverly Hills Playhouse, where I did the most intense and transformative acting work of my life! The acting classes were phenomenal…introspective and real, but also intense and exhausting. The master teacher was Milton Katselas, and he had three assistants - Jeffrey Tambor, Richard Lawson, and Gary Imhoff - who were all master teachers in their own right. My classmates and I were completely invested and committed. We had all traveled from across the country so that we could improve our acting. We were willing to work hard in the hopes of becoming respected actors. My class consisted of about 80 people, all talented artists. I didn't realize it at first, but Milton and many of my classmates and teachers were Scientologists. It wasn't forced down my throat, though, and they were all cool with me, so I had no qualms about it.

I had encountered Scientology once before. There was one occasion when I was invited to the Scientology celebrity center in Hollywood. I was greeted by a rep and then led to a room with a small theater with three other people so that we could all watch an introductory video. The video included a couple of Hollywood stars and the typical "this will change your life" stuff. I remember a point in the video where one of the host actors basically said, point blank, "If you don't join, you're just stupid", which definitely rubbed me the wrong way. I felt that it was very inappropriate. The introduction was followed by a 30 minute presentation by other members, who discussed a number of different concepts. I thought that some of the stuff that they presented was pretty useful and interesting.

After the presentation, I was brought to an office with two young members, and an older, senior member. The senior member had a big smile on her face and asked me what I thought of the video. I honestly told her that I disliked the condescending message at the end. She tried to make light of it, but she seemed taken aback by my blunt response. Hey, I'm a New Yorker; we don't put up with being persuaded to do something we really don't want to. The senior member tried to talk me into signing a contract with them, which I definitely was not comfortable with. At this point, I firmly explained that I was not interested and left the building. That was my one brief and strange encounter with Scientology.

Anyway, back at the Playhouse, it was all about putting up powerful work so that the teachers could give you notes on how you could improve as an actor. In each class, you would be asked to perform a scene, and you would work with an acting partner. Once you and your partner performed the scene, the other actors and the teacher would give you suggestions and comment on your work. This would provide you with the opportunity to enhance your abilities as an actor. When actors were emotionally tight, Milton might suggest doing a personal monologue or a song and dance exercise. He had different ways of helping us to loosen up so that we could really embody the character that we were playing in each of our scenes.

We were all required to memorize and understand what was called The Checklist, a list of various aspects of acting. Here is The Checklist, for those of you who are curious:

1. The Event

2. Evaluation

3. Behavior

4. Physical/Emotional State

5. The Moment before the Scene

6. Creative Hiding

7. Be a Person

8. Inner and Outer Life

9. The Cover

10. Who's the Author

11. Improvisation

12. Humor

13. Trust

14. Pathology

15. Objectives

When the teacher called out one of these points, the actor would immediately have a sense of what to do. For instance, "Evaluation" is about analyzing yourself and your presence in a scene. In Milton's words, "Am I on fire? Are the choices hot enough, alive? This scene is loaded. The stakes are high. Am I ready for that?" Think about it. We don't go to the movies to watch the basic, mundane, simple ins and outs of everyday life. Milton would refer to those basic and non-dramatic events as *cold*. We go to the movies to see drama and extraordinary circumstances play out. Milton referred to these big, dramatic events and feelings as *hot*. As an actor, you always want to look for what makes a scene hotter and more active. If the scene lacked fire and drama, the teacher might shout, "Evaluate higher!"

Of course, these points are easier said than done – you had to really work to make certain aspects of your performance come alive on stage. When it came to something like "The Cover", also called

Creative Hiding, you had to learn how to conceal your emotions. For example, sometimes in a relationship, you have to confront your partner or tell them something important. These moments can be sensitive and make you feel vulnerable, so you might avoid looking the other person in the eye. You might not be doing it on purpose; it can just be really difficult to look someone directly in the eye when you're dealing with something that is serious and intimate. If you can properly and naturally pull this off during a performance, it can make your performance more realistic. To achieve this, Milton would ask us to look out into the sunset instead of looking at our acting partner, or to concentrate our attention on a tablecloth or other inanimate objects.

I had both successes and flops in these classes. That's what I was there for, of course. You have to take chances and fall on your face sometimes. Some of my scenes really sucked and some of them got a thunderous standing ovation. In the same week, you might do both the best work of your life and the absolute worst. The best thing you can do in these classes is to play it fully out and make all of the mistakes you can, so that your teacher can help you. The entire process is really a process of self-discovery. You're finding out more about yourself and you're figuring out what roles would be the best fit for you. Once you're at a more advanced level, you should only perform scenes that fit your casting. Otherwise, you won't be cultivating your craft in a way that connects with people. Of course, if you just want to act and perform all types of roles, that's fine too. However, if you want to really connect with your audience, you should do work that fits you.

Jeffrey Tambor was a really fun teacher and he was able to make us laugh at his leisure. You might know Jeff from his roles on *The Larry Sanders Show*, *Arrested Development*, and *Transparent*. He critiqued the first scene that I put up during class. The scene was my own rendition of a scene from Shakespeare's *Othello*. I placed it in a modern day setting and I imagined Othello as a world champion boxer with Iago as Othello's manager, who betrays him and stabs him in the back. Jeffrey liked the idea, but he felt that I was acting more from an idea rather than from an experience of actually being betrayed. Milton quietly walked in during the scene and followed up with his own critique after Jeffrey gave his comments. He made me perform part of a scene with an actress who played Desdemona, Othello's tragic love interest. Milton directed me to be more intimate with her, to bring out the love in the scene and to have me really feel it. It was awesome. I learned a lot from Jeffrey and Milton's critiques and their comments truly helped me grow as an artist.

Milton had a real knack for gaining an actor's attention and trust. You really felt that he loved actors and knew exactly how to open them up. He wanted actors to be able to direct themselves, because we are not always going to have the luxury of receiving a director's full attention. One has to learn how to have the confidence to take the initiative and to direct one's own performance. Another important lesson from Milton was work ethic. He told us that if you're an actor on a set, you cannot get sick. It is important that you figure out how to stay healthy, that you find that herbal potion or concoction that kicks the flu's butt. This is because each day that you miss could cost the production hundreds of thousand dollars. He really taught us about the importance of a great work ethic and the need to show up to the set with a great attitude. Milton had many tools to help an actor to develop their technique and work ethic. Unfortunately, he passed away from heart failure in 2008, but I'll always remember his teachings.

One of my most memorable performances in class was a scene from *Glengarry Glen Ross*. I picked a number of other classmates to appear in the scene with me. I first picked one of the oldest guys at the Playhouse, Don Sullivan. He was a really nice and laid back guy who had experiences working in the old, early Hollywood Western films. He and I became friendly and had lunch many times, talking about scenes and laughing at the different things that occurred at the academy. He played the role played by Jack Lemmon, while I gave Ed Harris' role to a classmate who was a great actor and a really talented Venice Beach performer (he was known for juggling chainsaws and crazy things like that). Finally, I gave the role played by Kevin Spacey to a woman who worked for the Playhouse. She was the foreperson in the front office and she was sort of the enforcer of official rules, but she was also a very good actress.

I felt prepared going into rehearsal, but I got thrown when one of the actors started to improvise and argued with me in the scene. We all stayed in character, but it was so real that it confused me for a moment. I never forgot it, because it taught me that acting could be spontaneous and unplanned.

When it was time to put the scene up in class, I felt okay but I was nervous. I would be performing in front of around 80 professional actors in the class, all watching my work with a critical eye. Jeffrey Tambor was teaching that night. When I walked on stage with the woman who was playing Kevin Spacey's character, everyone began to chuckle. They were surprised to see a woman play a role that had been originally played by a man. We had good chemistry, but Jeffery stopped me after a few seconds. He had me do some martial arts strikes into the air so that I could loosen up. He really wanted me to own the scene and suggested that I add some martial arts moves into my performance. I was playing the role that Alec Baldwin played in the film, and the role certainly didn't call for any kung fu moves. But I knew that Jeffrey was right and I understood what he was trying to tell me; someone else had already put their mark on the performance, and I had to find something unique to make it my own. Jeffrey helped me through it and the performance became exactly that: my own.

I punctuated each of my lines with a big martial arts strike! My version went something like this:

"A, B, C. A - Always! B - Be! C - Closing! Always be closing! (strikes the air). Always be closing! (more fast strikes). A – I – D - A. Attention, Interest, Decision, Action. Attention…do I have your attention? Interest…are you interested? I know you are, because it's fuck or walk. You close or you hit the bricks (strikes the air)! Decision…have you made your decision for Christ? And Action (more fast strikes and a Bruce Lee-style martial arts shout). A, I, D, A. Get out there and do it!"

Thanks to the help of my fellow actors and Jeffrey's suggestions, I did really great work in class that day, and everyone loved it!

I developed good relationships with Milton, Jeffery and Richard. However, despite these connections, I didn't always feel like I was really a member of the Playhouse community. I took many classes there and I was involved in the Playhouse world for quite a while, but I always felt like an outsider. I felt like there was something wrong a lot the time, either with me or somebody else or my life in general. I felt uneasiness inside of me, but I didn't know what it was. It was like there was a glitch in my life. I yearned to be free from this confusion.

I simply didn't understand how I fit into the Hollywood community, and a lot of the time I just felt alone and alienated. I used to tell myself that my brother was the one who was good in community situations, not me. I needed to find the power to integrate myself into communities, but I didn't find it until much later. Of course, that was just a story that I had convinced myself was true. I eventually realized that I couldn't let any old ideas or insecurities block up my potential or prevent me from becoming a better, more enlightened person!

The Sweet Science

If I could take my pain and put it on a canvas, it would look a little something like this...

Left hooks rolling off my shoulder and hard

I'm pulling to the 4 sides, throwing till I win the cigar

Float like a butterfly sting like a bee, wooahh, come on, try and catch me

Your jabs bouncing off my head all I can do is fight and wish you were dead

Come on suck it up and work your way back in

Bite down on your mouthpiece he's not your fucking friend

Make him your bitch to be sewn up stitch by stitch

Put his ribs on a plate cause you're broke and need to eat

I'm here for the takin', fakin', bakin' under the lights and all this heat

Let's get ready to rumble as I stumble back to my feet for

Another chance to put asleep defeat

I could've been a contender

Fuck that

Kick his ass so hard he grabs his head

Step by step, inch by inch, behold the power of a

master

Cause I was looking for love in all the wrong places

I'm in the bloody ring

Spitting my membranes into a bucket till the bell

goes ding

Bobbing and weaving until I get the judges call

They love me, they really love me,

Split decision? What's the call?

A draw?

No, I want more seeing his ass on the canvas floor

I want a knock out so everyone can see I'm a master

at work

You know they paid to see me

I can't go back home and tell my boys that I lost No

way, I'm the man they got to know that I'm boss I

fought to the death like a real man should

Even my mama said, "If he puts his hands on you,

make sure to make him pay"

So stay tuned for more sweet science, as I said, you
will see

I could kick some ass, maybe two or even three On
the canvas I lay the laws

Sweat, funk, dirty showers and dirty draws

Man this is insane

I thought love was the only pleasure that was worth
so much pain

Chapter 11 - The Hollywood Ecosystem

*"If you want a happy life…that depends, of course,
on where you stop your story."*

Orson Welles

When you're training for an important fight, you meet a lot of people who are also training for greatness. Some of those people won't be able to keep up with your intensity and dedication, while some will be your equal, while others will be on a completely different level, forcing you to work harder so that you can catch up to them. I've been lucky, because I've met so many people who have both challenged and encouraged me.

When I was in Hollywood, though, it was a struggle to make those important connections with people. The more I look at the past and think about who I was and who Hollywood wanted me to be, I see that I was very naïve and that I didn't understand the dynamics in that city. I was approaching things from an individual perspective, as a talent that wanted and deserved a certain level of respect and success. I was looking to be "recognized." I was wrong, and I needed to put myself out there to meet people and create the community that I needed to support me.

If you want to get work in Hollywood, it's all about who you know, and getting to know people means that you have to have great social skills. You have to know how to behave within the dynamics of Hollywood. You have to be a politician. If you burn a bridge, you have to understand who you're burning a bridge with and you have to know how to make amends. It takes humility, perseverance, dedication, a clear mind, and patience.

In the late 90's, I met Brian Austin Green of *Beverly Hills 90210*. He recognized me at an event we were both attending and told me he wanted to get into kickboxing. I was living in Hollywood at the time and he lived a little up the hill, not too far from me. He had a nice house and we began to train at his place. He had the eye of the tiger and wanted to learn how to fight. I liked that eagerness about him. He was learning some really good techniques and I think he was getting a lot out of the training. It wasn't just about what he was physically learning – I could tell that it was having a strong mental effect on him as well.

After I got Brian proficient enough, we began to do some light sparring. Sometimes, we brought in a friend of ours, a trainer from Crunch Gym, Stephen Bishop, who is now an actor. I had them spar, though nothing too heavy. We weren't in a ring and I didn't want them getting hurt. It was quite amusing watching their personalities clash. The testosterone in the room was deafening. They'd go at it and then argue with one another when one of them went too far. The rule was that they wouldn't go any harder than about 70%. Teaching was a good time for me.

I have great memories with both of them and they were good guys. Brian even reached out to *90210*'s casting department and arranged for me to meet with them. They gave me a small role where I just played a bartender in the background. When I got called onto the set of the show, they gave me a little dressing room and I was on the same floor as Brian and most of the other male actors, like Jason Priestly, Luke Perry, and Ian Ziering. Brian introduced me, explaining that I was his boxing coach, and they were all very nice to me. Some of the other background actors and extras recognized me and were really excited to meet me, but the producer and director were really busy and didn't notice that I had that kind of love out there. The director probably didn't know anything about me at all, except that I was an actor behind a bar on his set.

The *90210* producers called me back to play the bartender a few more times. It was a nice experience but I felt underutilized. When fans on the set recognized me, they repeatedly told me how much they were impacted by *The Last Dragon*…they revealed their hopes and dreams to me. Many explained that they'd seen the movie a gazzilion times. I heard that over and over, and I had hoped that the director and producers would hear it too.

I took a lot of other small roles where I experienced similar encounters. The extras on the set would show me love, but the casting either didn't know me or wasn't informed about who I was. I think that a big issue was that I didn't have a powerful representation. One of the most difficult things for me was to accept that I wasn't getting recognition by the industry for who I was as an actor and performer. I had been the star of a major motion picture and had fans everywhere I went. Fans may think that that's great, but if you're not on a casting director's radar, you're just not going to get noticed. From Hollywood's point of view, I was just another actor trying to get a nut, trying to be recognized in a big pool of wannabes. In a way, that was true. With everything I know now, I see how it was a losing struggle. I needed to learn so much more about myself before I could continue to achieve success in any field.

I stayed in Hollywood through the end of 2001. Before I left, I got a call from my friend Tony Selznick, who was the co-owner of MSA, a successful dance agency. He told me that Madonna was interested in working with me. She wanted me to teach her martial arts and choreograph some numbers for her upcoming "Drowned World" tour. It was an exciting opportunity to do something quite cool and unique.

Madonna may have heard of me from the music video choreography that I did for Gavin Rossdale and his band Bush. It was the video for their song "Chemicals Between Us" – I hired all of the martial artists for the video, choreographed their moves, and even had a brief role as the masked samurai who battles Gavin. The video was artistic and cool, and it was such a great thing to add to my resume. Here's a funny story about that video: there was this one guy who could do some really nice kicks, but he didn't know how to follow directions. He was what you would call a loose cannon. He would throw kicks all the time, even when the camera wasn't on him, and he constantly acted like a madman, trying to get attention. If you look up the video, you'll see him in the background, kicking like crazy when the monk is demonstrating his kung fu.

I went to the valley to meet with Madonna's dance choreographer, Jamie King, and I eventually met with Madonna herself to discuss what she wanted to achieve. It all went smoothly and she was really cool with me. I took her and her husband, Guy Richie, to Marcos Vinicius' jiu-jitsu school in Beverly Hills, where they started to learn the basics of jiu-jitsu technique. Richie would later continue training with Marcos, and he even reached the level of brown belt.

I taught Madonna the basic martial arts moves that I wanted her to do in the show, and she picked up things pretty quickly. She had such a vast dance background which made things a lot easier. We began working on the choreography at Paramount Studios. It was a pretty big job so I hired an assistant, another martial artist who I knew. We began working on the number for her song, "Sky Fits Heaven," and it went really well at first. After a short time, though, things got a little tense when I saw other choreographers being fired. Madonna wanted everything to be a certain way; if she didn't think someone was pulling their weight or she didn't have chemistry with certain choreographers, they were gone, even if they had impressive professional backgrounds and a lot of experience.

Eventually, I started to notice that my assistant was acting very strangely. I also noticed that some of the people on the set were acting oddly towards me too, for no apparent reason. I sensed that something underhanded was happening behind my back. Russell Clark, who worked for Tony Selznick's MSA agency, soon contacted me about these issues. Russell was a well-known choreographer in Hollywood and he was a great family friend. He was sort of like an uncle to me. He hinted to me that something was going on, but he wanted me to investigate and figure it out for myself. I soon realized that my assistant was trying to undermine my authority with Jaime King and the other choreographers - when I showed moves to Jamie or anyone else, my assistant would subtly challenge my style or question my techniques. He was also talking behind my back and spreading rumors about me. Yes, my assistant was trying to steal my job.

Madonna only came in to work, and never hung out, so she didn't know anything was amiss. She worked well with me and since I was still on the job, I knew things were cool, but that wouldn't last for long if I didn't solve this problem. Although some damage was already done to my relationships with the people in charge, I kept my cool. I went home, emailed my assistant, and told him that he was fired. I dropped him without an explanation. When someone is behaving in such a low way, they don't deserve an explanation or my friendship any longer. I finished the job alone…it came out great, and Madonna was really happy.

I was so naïve, so much like Bruce Leroy, though I didn't realize it until I was much older. While the surface of the entertainment business is very glamorous, behind the scenes, there are all kinds of dirty folks with no integrity, trying to do whatever they can to get ahead. You've got to watch your back all the time and it's difficult to trust people. I would have to fail many, many more times before my eyes could open wider and I could fully appreciate all of the opportunities that were right in front of me.

The whole entertainment business can really be a lonely place. You have many people around you, but many are so-called friends, moochers, and weirdoes, and it can feel lonely and isolating. It's hard to know who to trust, and many relationships feel false and inauthentic. When you have a real relationship, you need to hold onto it and cherish it, because you never know when it might end.

One night, I got a call from Russell Clark. His voice was weak and I could hear fear behind his words. He said, "Taimak, I've been diagnosed with cancer." I only lived a few blocks from him, so I ran over to his place. It was a shock to me - he had been given only a few months to live. At the time I didn't have the emotional facilities to deal with something like this, especially since it was happening to someone who was so close to me. I just felt numb and completely shaken to my core. For about a week, I helped him get in and out of bed, and I even had to help him to the bathroom. He was dying right in front of me. His sister and mom eventually came and helped, and also hired a professional caretaker.

Russell had a lot of pride and he was an extremely self-driven, intelligent and responsible man. He had a great sense of humor. He was loving and generous. He was a talented artist. All of his friends loved him and he was a great person. He lived his life with so much energy and passion, and I know that it was difficult and embarrassing for him to be cared for by other people. But, like everything in his life, he handled himself with grace and dignity. After Russell passed, I came back to New York City. I felt like a bit of a failure. Like so many young actors, I went to Los Angeles with high hopes, but came home empty.

Russell's death was like the straw that broke the camel's back. I was in Hollywood for around four years, and like so many in that city, I had just had it. I was done, like a piece of burnt toast. I was done with the plastic environment, the lying, the cheating, struggling to make ends meet, and just generally the whole feeling of not connecting with myself at all. I needed to start doing some serious acting roles, and it wasn't just about making money. It was to express all of the complicated emotions that I was feeling. I needed to get out there and just explode, letting go of all of my frustration and anxiety.

In 2004, I was cast to play the lead role in an Off-Broadway adaptation of Patrick Swayze's cult classic film *Roadhouse*. *Roadhouse* is a cult movie because people feel that "it's so bad, it's good." I played an internationally revered bouncer who was hired to clean up a small town dive, only to get sucked into the messy and corrupt local politics. My character bit off more than he could chew – or did he? After all, what problems couldn't be solved by a few well-timed roundhouse kicks?

I wore a blond mullet wig for the role and everyone loved the look. It was a riot and so fun to do. The show brought out not only the *Roadhouse* fans, but fans of *The Last Dragon* as well. It was a hit and people responded really well to it! The production was hilarious and survived a really rough year in the aggressive New York theater scene. The show had a nice little run and to this day, people still tell me how much they enjoyed it.

Doing live theater can be a scary, but also fun and exciting thing because you never know what's gonna happen. During the run of the show we would sometimes do two performances in a single day. The cast was fun and would goof around a lot; sometimes that worked out and sometimes, it didn't. This one particular time Rachel and I we're about to go on-stage and do a love scene.

There was supposed to be a bed and some furniture set up on stage before the scene (during this time the actors also acted as stage hands so some of the cast were responsible for setting this scene). The lights were off and it was dark; Rachel and I were in position to go on stage. Just then, the lights went back on and there wasn't any furniture on the set. Now, in theater a lot of times you just have to improvise, you don't have the luxury of complaining, so Rachel and I went onto the bare stage ready to make love on a bed that wasn't there. It was awkward at first.

I grabbed her and we began to kiss. I placed her on the floor, we began to kiss there and then as I was on top of her I held onto her and we rolled across the stage; Rachel was great, she just went with it! As we got to the other side of the stage I said, "Let's roll back!" We then barrel rolled back the other way; It worked! The audience was falling off their seats with laughter. Who needs a bed when you have a leading lady like Rachel?

While writing this book, I spoke with Rachel and we reminisced about the good times doing Roadhouse. She offered this about her experience:

> *From our first meeting I was incredibly impressed with Taimak's physical grace, confidence and kindness.*

Taimak was absolutely great on stage. This play could easily have become very campy very quickly and Taimak really led the way in playing it straight and true to the characters presented. He was a great leading man who actually led the cast on stage and off. Instead of being overly dramatic or goofing off in rehearsals and on stage, Taimak was always incredibly focused and present. He delivered the all his lines, including "Pain don't hurt", with absolute sincerity and could go from 0-60 when a huge fight scene jumped off.

At one point in the show, Dalton is being seduced by Dr. Clay (my character) and Taimak would follow me down a set of stairs on the front of the stage and into the audience. As Dr. Clay, I would pick out a guy from the audience and sit on his lap. Taimak would lean in to give me a kiss but would actually go for the guys who's lap I was sitting on. Just before he was going to touch lips with a male audience member he would realize his "mistake" and kiss me instead. I once got kicked in the leg really hard by a jealous girlfriend as I was sitting on her boyfriends lap. She didn't like Taimak trying to kiss him either. But don't worry, I kicked her back before Taimak lifted me back onstage.

Taimak's unlike any actor I've every worked with. He had an intense stillness about him on stage that radiates his confidence and strength. He's always very physically and mentally present and when he looks at you, you feel like you're the center of the universe.

As the fight choreographer of Road House, Taimak came up with incredible fight scenes that would involve the entire cast of 12 actors and included breaking beer bottles over heads, throwing people off the stage and characters getting hit so hard that the actors flew backwards 10 feet in the air. He always pushed me to do more, be more, and to get stronger. Before shows he would single me out and make do crunches and leg lifts till I could barely move. Then laugh playfully as I hobbled up to take the stage.

It was an absolute blast working with Taimak and watching him perform on stage and I hope to some day see him on stage again!"

The *Roadhouse* director, Timothy Haskell, later cast me in another one of his plays. It was called *Last Life*, and it was a musical that mixed in martial arts choreography – a "fightsical"! Haskell conceived of the project with writer Eric Sanders, and it was a really unique piece. In their words, the play takes place "in a borderless, burnt out world, [where] the few remaining inhabitants were at the end of a long and indefinable war. The survivors, not knowing what they are even fighting for, vow to destroy each other and wrest control of what remains." *Last Life* opened at The Brick Theater in Brooklyn, and then it got extended and moved to Manhattan at The Ohio Theater.

I thought that Haskell was such an imaginative director, and it was an incredible experience to work with him. He had a truly unique sense of humor in his work, which I really appreciated and enjoyed. He was able to take something like a seemingly simple action drama and coat it with irony and humor, and he wanted me to add to this rich texture by helping him to create some intense fight scenes. As great as *Last Life* was, Haskell is still probably better known as the creator and director of Nightmare: New York's Most Horrifying Haunted House, as well as the Nightmare Horror Show: New York's Most Terrifying Theater Festival, which happens every year.

I soon took a few other theater roles and I was eventually cast to work in a play with a bunch of other black celebs, including an R&B singer and various TV personalities. It was a national tour that was already up and running, and I was cast as a replacement for one of the lead roles. I was happy to have booked the gig, but I had recently strained my back and had to ice it every day. I was going to be doing a physical scene in the play, and I would need to put myself through constant therapy to make sure that I was properly healed.

I was flown out to the theater and my job at first was simply to watch the show and become familiar with it. I needed to learn the staging and the blocking, and I had to observe how the characters interacted with each other. I would take over the part in the next few days and was told to prepare by asking the other actors to go over scenes with me to get some practice in. However, I wasn't received very well by the lead actor who was also one of the producers. When I introduced myself to him, he looked away, left me hanging and then walked away. For a second I thought he didn't hear me say hello to him, but he continued to display these kinds of behaviors. For example, there was a time where we wound up in the same elevator of our hotel. I said hello again, but he ignored me completely and then got off. I didn't know where the animosity was coming from. I felt like it began to influence how some of the group was being with me, as if I was invading their space. I just didn't understand where the hate came from.

On the day of my first show, one of the actors, who I previously worked with when we were younger, came up to my room and wished me luck. It was the last time that we really spoke. I didn't perform well in that first show. I had problems with my lines and the blocking. I didn't feel like anybody was open to helping me; we didn't do a run-through before I actually went up to do the show. In most professional shows, this is standard procedure. I told the producer many times that I wanted to do a run-through but he never gave me that opportunity. It was unprofessional but there was nothing I could do about it.

Afterwards, all of the cast members sat me down during a break and asked me about the role I was playing. It seemed like they wanted to help, but they all directed the blame of my poor performance solely to me. I felt they were being unfair, and got pretty defensive. They had rehearsed the show together for several weeks before their first performance, whereas I never got the opportunity to do a single run-through, despite my many pleas to do so. On top of that, they had a lot of time to build up the group chemistry that they had, which I never could. I felt real shitty about the whole situation, which lead to a bit of an argument with them - after that, they never helped me again. If this happened today, I know to handle the situation in a very different way, but back then I was sensitive.

The rest of the cast went out and partied after each show. I didn't join them and they assumed that I was trying to avoid them. In reality, it was a physical problem with my back that I mentioned earlier. Because of the physicality of the role, my back was in pain during and after every show. After each performance, I would quickly return to my hotel room and ice my back; there was always another show that same night or the following day, and my body needed to recover. In the end, there was a lot of miscommunication and hurt feelings – I guess that's what happens when everyone is too wrapped up in their egos, and we are too proud to simply reach out and connect with each other.

Some of the cast gradually became openly hostile with me, and it was pretty uncomfortable to perform with some of them. The lead actor began changing his lines while we were doing the show, right on stage, in front of the audience. He was cracking on me and trying to put me down. He was a really ignorant type of guy and he would say things like, "You know you light-skinned niggas think you're all that." He somehow kept all of the other actors on his side. He was one of the producers of the show and I assumed that they didn't want to lose their jobs, so they just went along. I just had to deal with it. I knew I had a job to do, and I wasn't going to let these guys get in my way.

The other producer of the show eventually came into town to see what was going on. Some of the cast lied to him and told him that

I was doing a horrible job. They really were out to get me. When I went up on stage that night, with the producer in the audience, I gave it my all and really nailed the role. I started getting better and better as the show went on, and before long I was able to really make the role my own. In the end, the run of the show was a great success and it did quite well.

One of the strangest relationships I formed with a cast member was with a good looking actress who was also a little out of her mind. She gave me a really hard time. She constantly put me down and tried to turn the group against me every chance she got. She said some ugly things to me, over and over and again, but I did my best to ignore it and her. I was getting paid well and I just told myself that I needed to take it day by day. It was strange, though, because she would also hit on me. I didn't want to have anything to do with her at that point, but I had to admit that we had an odd attraction for each other. After our final show, we all had dinner together and went back to the hotel. She and I got off the elevator and it seemed like we were going to head to our respective rooms. Instead, she followed me to my door and grabbed the door knob as I started to go inside. She shoved me into my room. She grabbed me and kissed me and I kissed her back. We had a wild time that night.

Sometimes, your biggest enemy can become somewhat of a friend, all in one passionate moment. One second someone hates you and the very next they're all over you. I've had many different relationships with women over the years, and these relationships have never been simple. That's what makes life interesting, I guess.

Chapter 12 - The Game of Love

"In love, it always seems like there's some piece missing, like solving a puzzle, but it doesn't work that way. Give all of yourself to it or nothing at all."

My personal motto

Not too long ago, I was cleaning out one of my closets with the help of my little niece, Skyla. She noticed my framed poster of *The Last Dragon* and immediately pointed to the image of Denise. She asked, "Who is that?" It's funny...whenever I've had a woman in my life, whether it be a professional or a personal relationship, my family is always grilling me to know every detail and to learn more about these ladies. This chapter is about the various relationships I've had with women over the years. These stories are crazy, emotional, and bittersweet, and I hope that they can teach you something about life and love. I know that I've definitely learned from these experiences.

My first really serious relationship was with a girl named Veronica. I first met Veronica when we were both kids. She was trapped in an abusive relationship with a much older man named Ike. He was an extremely creepy sexual predator who was in his mid-50's. The crazy thing was that her mom actually approved of their relationship and encouraged it. Ike was a millionaire and paid for everything that

Veronica's mom needed - the house payment, cars, clothes, food, absolutely everything. Veronica's dad had abandoned the family and gone off with another woman, so her mom must have thought that Ike was a blessing in her time of need. All she needed to do was to turn a blind eye to her daughter's exploitation. She wasn't happy about Veronica's relationship with me; if Veronica refused to see Ike, it would mean the end of their meal ticket. Veronica was confused about the whole thing and didn't know what to do.

Eventually, Veronica and I decided to get serious and I helped her run away from this terrible situation. We rented a place in Queens and Veronica cut off all contact with Ike and her mom. It wasn't all smooth sailing, though. Ike kept trying to contact Veronica and her mom tried to manipulate her into coming back to him. Veronica wanted to make her mom happy and she started to tell me that Ike wasn't really a bad person, after all. I got really frustrated and I didn't know how to talk to her about it. At the same time, I was feeling a lot of anxiety about my career, and that really affected my mood as well. I needed a change of scenery and I needed to do something fresh. I eventually got the opportunity to go to California to be a guest star on the show *A Different World*. This was the perfect chance to do something new...I wanted a break from the New York scene and this was my ticket. However, Veronica wasn't happy about it. She was extremely vulnerable and I could see her heart aching when I told her about going to California. She felt like I was leaving her, and in a way I was. I wanted to get away and do my own thing for a bit. We were both young and it was simply an overwhelming situation.

I did a good job on the show and it was a nice experience for me. I decided to stay in Los Angeles for a while and do more work. At first, I spoke with Veronica almost every day. That didn't last long, though. I started to make excuses and only called her once or twice a week. I ended up meeting other girls; I cheated on her and lied to her. A few weeks went by and then, a few weeks turned into a few months. Veronica knew it was done. I didn't really want our relationship to end because I still had feelings for her, and I tried to keep her. But when I didn't hear from her for over a week and she stopped returning my calls, I knew something was going on. I didn't know how to deal with the fact that she was leaving me - after all, we had been passionately in love at one time. She started seeing another guy and it seemed like things were really over between us.

It was around this time that I starred in *The White Girl* and met Troy Byer. During the production of the film, Troy and I began dating. We were young, having fun and we were the stars of the movie, so it made sense. We were also connected in a way, because our mothers were friends with each other. Troy and I were very different, though... she was originally from New York, but had transplanted herself to Hollywood and enjoyed the glamorous Hollywood lifestyle. I was a more down-to-earth New York type of guy. When the movie finished filming, I went back to New York and Troy went back to California. As I mentioned earlier, my mom knew her mom, so Troy knew a bit about my past and she knew that I was a bit distant at that point in my life. She wanted me to open up because she felt that I was in love with her, but the truth was that I still had feelings for Veronica.

I decided that Veronica and I should give our relationship another chance and I didn't see Troy again for several months.

I was out at work one day and I unexpectedly got a call from my mom; someone was paying her a visit and this person was waiting for me to show up. When I came back home, Troy was there. She had shown up with her girlfriend, an actress named Tia Carrere. They were sitting in the living room with Veronica, who was staying with me. Troy asked a lot of questions and she wanted to know a lot about Veronica - she kept pumping Veronica for some personal information. I knew that Veronica was fuming inside and wanted to beat Troy up, but she kept her calm. Troy was all smiles and playing friendly, although I'm sure she could tell that I wasn't happy with her surprise visit. She didn't care about how I felt, though. She just wanted to cause a scene. After a while, Veronica ran upstairs and I quickly went after her. I spoke to her and tried to calm her down. Veronica understood that my relationship with Troy was over, so she finally relaxed.

After that dramatic day, Veronica and I continued to date, but our relationship didn't go so well. We continually declared that we needed to go our separate ways. But it's never quite that simple, is it? Veronica and I always wound up getting back together, and we went back and forth like that for the next three and half years. We had really strong feelings for each other and we just couldn't stay away. Eventually, the pain of it all was just wearing on the both of us... breaking up, making up, breaking up, making up, again and again. It was stressful and exhausting

Whenever Veronica and I broke up, I would play the field and meet other girls. I started going out with the actress Lisa Bonet who was starring in *The Cosby Show* at the time. We had a good time together. However, I just didn't have the maturity to handle a serious relationship. I was meeting a lot of girls and I was cocky. I wouldn't necessarily say that I was a player - that wasn't my style - but I was immature. I liked Lisa, but I was young and had no idea how to be with her. I didn't want to hurt her and I broke it off with her. A few years later, during another separation from Veronica, I dated Carmen Electra. When I was around Carmen, it was like I was showing off and I thought it was good attention for me. In the end, I found out that Carmen was seeing someone else at the same time. She was surprised that I didn't know about her other guy - apparently it was all over the tabloids, but I don't follow the gossip. Carmen and I stopped dating...it just couldn't work out.

As the years went by, Veronica and I kept trying to make our relationship work. In the end, we decided to call it quits for the last time. I eventually ended up falling in love with someone else. I met up with a friend at a popular restaurant and bar called The Coffee Shop in downtown Manhattan, and I saw this beautiful girl. Her name was Michol and she was half Spanish and half German. We were immediately attracted to one another. She was easy going, had an infectious smile, and was just perfect in every way. Michol and I grew closer and we had so much fun together. It was great time for us as a couple and for me as a person. It was a refreshing feeling after coming out of such a tumultuous relationship with Veronica. We were really happy and the months quickly passed by. I completely forgot about Veronica and I never heard from her.

Around this time, I was hanging out with a couple of guys named Cliff and Shazi. Cliff was a chiropractor and Shazi had a thriving photo lab business. They rented a triplex apartment on Madison Avenue and they were constantly throwing big parties. Cliff and Shazi actually knew Veronica and also knew about our dysfunctional relationship together. Veronica would occasionally swing by Cliff's office to ask questions about me. After these little interrogations, Cliff would call me up and say, "Hey Tai, sheeeee's baaaack!" Cliff used to tease me all the time about it. He believed that she was furious about my new relationship with Michol.

One night, Cliff and Shazi threw a big party. Music was playing throughout their entire pad, upstairs and downstairs, the whole place was jumping with people, booze, and a lot of energy. All of sudden, I saw Cliff coming towards me with a funny look on his face. He explained that Veronica was in the building, was pretty drunk, and he was worried about what she would do or say. I didn't pay any attention...it was a huge apartment and she might not even notice me. I chilled with Michol and the time flew by. We were lying down on this huge couch, just chatting and hanging out together. Suddenly, I looked to my right and there was Veronica, lying down next to us with a huge smile on her face.

Michol asked me who she was. I lied and told her that I didn't know. I just said that I was going to make her go away. I got up and took Veronica by her arm into the hallway. Veronica was drunk. She fell to her knees and started crying and yelling, asking me why I didn't love her anymore. I explained that I had a new girlfriend. I asked her to leave me alone and explained that I had cried enough tears over her. I left the party with Michol and went home, assuming that this was a freak meeting and that it wasn't going to have any effect on me.

Unfortunately, I underestimated my feelings. I still had Veronica's residue within me and I still had deep feelings for her. Veronica eventually came to see me and we kept getting together. I thought to myself, "Maybe I'm not really in love with Michol?" I broke up with Michol at this point because I thought that was the right thing to do. Ultimately, though, things didn't work out with Veronica. Did I do the right thing? The one thing I know for sure is, just because you have feelings for someone and want to be with them, it doesn't mean that everything will work out the way you want it to.

Fast-forward almost 15 years - around this time, I was dating a really nice Dominican girl named Natalia. She was a sprinter and a model, and we had a great time together. We dated for about a year but ultimately broke it off and just became friends. We would talk on the phone once in a while and regularly update each other (this detail will be important in a little bit). After our relationship was over and I was enjoying the single life, I suddenly got an email from a woman through Facebook which read "Hey, how are you! It's been so long." She explained that she had met me in Los Angeles and wanted to know how I had been doing since then. I didn't remember her, but she was pretty and there was definitely something familiar about her. Her name was Sally – or, at least, that's what I'll call her in this book (I think it's best to withhold her real name). She was a champion fighter in martial arts and I was certainly impressed with her skill level and all that she had accomplished. My interest was sparked and I kept trying to figure out how she knew me. I emailed her back and she asked for my number.

We decided to stay in touch and talk more. Things went fast and we began to talk almost every day. We talked about many things over the next few weeks, as if we were already dating. We were both getting close and kind of intimate in these conversations. We decided to date and she made plans to come out to see me in New York. She bought a plane ticket, but right before she arrived, there was a red flag. She showed signs of having a nasty temper. She would especially get super riled up about my Facebook page, and began negatively responding to all the women who had commented on my pictures. I was taken aback, but due to the time I had invested and the commitment we had made, I ignored it. She went back and forth about whether she should come or not. I didn't do anything about it and I kept my pictures up. I agreed that I still wanted to meet her in person and we would see how it went.

When she visited, we clicked, and we continued to travel back and forth across the country to see each other. It was a difficult relationship, though. One moment, she was spectacular, loving, and fun to be with and then in the very next, she was manipulative and at times she got physical, which was the worst part. If I threatened to leave her, she would threaten to kill herself. If I didn't believe her, she would put a knife to her throat to test me. When we weren't together, she needed to speak to me every night because of her jealousy and her fear that there might be another woman lingering in the background while she wasn't there. She was upset that I still had a friendly relationship with Natalia and she would blow up with anger whenever she found out that I had spoken with Natalia on the phone. She made me promise that I would stop calling Natalia and that I wouldn't take her calls. I didn't want to agree, but I finally caved. It wasn't fair to Natalia – we were friends and there was nothing going on between us. But I simply couldn't deal with Sally's jealousy and constant accusations. The whole thing was exhausting. I was getting more and more distant from myself and who I really was and I felt like I was losing my mind. One night, before I went to sleep, I imagined a gun to my head…that was when I realized that I had to get out of this situation.

It all came to a head when I was staying with her in California. When I woke up one day, she was already upset. She accused me of talking to Natalia again, and she was becoming more and more agitated. I had agreed not to call Natalia and I had stuck by that promise. Her attitude was completely the result of her own paranoia. I tried to reassure her that she was imagining things and that I hadn't lied to her, but she refused to believe me. She eventually started charging at me and hitting me and I literally thought that my life was at stake. Remember, she was a very skilled martial artist and she was properly trained in how to hurt and disable people. She kept hitting me but I didn't hit her back. I knew that retaliating and hitting her would only give her a reason to really do something awful.

She got on the phone and called someone. She lied to whoever it was on the other end, telling them that I was attacking her. I tried to grab the phone from her but she wouldn't let go of it. I knew I had to get my stuff and get out of there before she convinced some friends to come over and attack me. She was out of her mind and I couldn't take any chances. All the while, she continued to hit me. I just made sure to protect my face and I let her hit me in the chest, arms and legs. She noticed that I was going for my clothes and my laptop, which were in an open suitcase. I had just started working on another script and wasn't finished with it - all of my hard work was on that computer. She started to grab my things and threw them all over the place. There was a chance that she could destroy that computer and erase months of work. I looked for my phone and called the police. She said, "Don't call the police stupid".

She headed to the door and screamed for her neighbors. Three guys came to the door and I was worried that they were going to be on her side and was not going to hear my side of things. I was quite afraid of what was going to happen, and we all stood there for a few seconds…it was extremely tense. Eventually, Sally began to shout, "He hit me!" while I responded with, "You're a liar!" The neighbor asked angrily, "What's going on, man?" I explained to him, "We're arguing, but I'm not hitting her, she's hitting me." I felt betrayed.

At this time the cops arrived and spoke to us separately. Noticing that I had scratches all over my chest and neck, they asked me if she had hit me, but I said no. I knew that if I said yes, there was the potential that they might file charges against her. Even after everything she had done, I still didn't want her to get into that kind of trouble. I just wanted them to let me get my things together so I could get out of there, but I didn't know anything about domestic violence laws in

California. Before I knew it, they turned me around and cuffed me. I was in shock. I asked them, "Why are you doing this? I was the one who called you to help me." They said that even though Sally didn't tell them that I had hit her, they had to arrest someone because it was a domestic violence call. That was the law.

They put me in the patrol car and took me to jail. There were no words: I was heartbroken. I looked out the window of the patrol car and saw her standing there, staring at me. Her face was blank. I'll never forget it. She looked shocked…she just stared at me, dumbfounded. I was a complete wreck.

I knew that someone would recognize me at the jailhouse. I didn't want anyone to recognize me and I felt really bad. Sure enough, I wasn't in the building for more than a couple of minutes when I was recognized by the woman who checked me in. She said, "Oh my God, what are you doing here?" I answered, "I'm dating this girl, she got me in here." She looked at me, sighed and said, "I've seen everybody in here." The guards began to recognize me as well. They were all surprised, but were also very nice to me. One of them was especially kind. He told me his whole family loved *The Last Dragon* and that he felt bad that I had to go through this. I was, of course, embarrassed and humiliated. I thought, this can't be my life, but it was. And when I had to change into jailhouse clothing, reality really hit me. I was spending the night in a jail and I didn't know when I would be able to get out.

I was taken up to the main holding area. I walked into the communal room. It was a large space, and there were a few tables where guys were sitting down talking or playing cards. Above, circling the area, were the cells where we would be lodging. There was a 24" TV, but it was high up on the wall, probably 15 feet up, so it was difficult to make out what was playing on the screen. I felt uncomfortable and awkward, but I tried to get as calm and collected as I could. I walked over to one of the tables and sat down. I introduced myself to the three guys there, and they did the same. I didn't let them know I was an actor and I don't believe they recognized me.

I talked a little, but I mostly listened to everybody else talk. I was trying to get a sense of their backgrounds. Two of them were drug dealers and the other guy stole cars. After a while, a big horn went off, signaling that we had to go into our cells. My spirit was broken as I walked up the stairs to my cell. My "roommate" was already in the cell. He was a small Mexican guy, who acted cool. I asked what he was in for and he said in a Mexican accent, "Selling weed." I smiled and asked, "Do you have any on you now?" We chuckled and got ready for bed. I took the top bunk and he took the bottom.

The horn went off again, waking me up. It must've been about midnight or close to it. Someone opened up my cell door and told me that I was going to be released. I was happily surprised and rushed out of the cell. I didn't know who had posted my bail and got me released. I checked my phone and saw that my friend Brenda had called. I called her back and she told me that it was Sally who came up with the money to release me, something like $3,000. Sally came to the jailhouse to pick me up and she tried to talk to me, but I just didn't respond to her. I couldn't believe that she had done this to me.

I had been hoping that my family wouldn't find out about this whole mess. Unfortunately for me, TMZ reported on their show that I was arrested for domestic abuse. They either keep tabs on the jail, or perhaps Sally's neighbors called them or maybe she did. My heart hit the ground. I never had to deal with anything like this in my life. I hit rock bottom and got depressed. My relationship with Sally was definitely over…or was it?

Believe it or not, I gave her one last chance. I know…what was I thinking? I was having a difficult relationship with my sister at the time, and Sally took advantage of that to create drama and turn my sister against me. She would text lies to my sister, telling her that I was abusive and that I had been beating her. When I finally saw the texts and realized what she was doing, I finally told her to leave. I've never met anyone who lied so much.

I gave her enough cab fare so that she could get to the airport for a flight back to LA. While she was at the airport, she texted me pictures of herself in a fetal position. I couldn't believe it…fetal position selfies! And at the same time, she was still texting my sister. I had to call my sister and ask her to not respond to her messages. I explained to her that she was a lunatic, and everything she said was simply not true. That day was the very end and there was never gonna be a sequel. It was over!

I really wanted to share these stories with you and openly discuss these difficult relationships. I hope that you'll be able to learn from the mistakes that I've made. These stories may lead you to believe that I regret my relationship with Sally or that I regret the mistakes

I've made with other women. However, I never regret anything in my life anymore. I used to regret things all the time, but I realized that just made me feel like I was walking around like an incomplete person. You can't change what has already taken place, but you can learn from it. You can put it in your box of tools and never forget it. Just take it with you on your personal journey, and continue to move forward in life.

There was a quote in The Last Dragon about being overly ambitious. It went like this,

"The secret awaits eyes unclouded by ambition, those bound by desire see only that which can be held in their hands." Another woman I dated for a brief time motivated me to write this about her.

Material Girl

Ahh, the almighty dollar, that's all you really crave

Having no time scrambling for your chances to your
very ending grave

It's so wonderful that Benz that phat ass Lexus too

Gowns diamonds and pearls jettin' to Park Avenue

Tom Dick or Harry, who cares, it's dollars I seek

From every credulous man that craves me, squat
down and kiss my feet

I'm fly aren't I, gorgeous too

You keep on telling me, I'll shave my tata for you

That's right I'm pink universe I'm master over you

I'm your Allah, your Buddha, your Jesus, silly fool

Cuz loving me is loving, don't you see it, silly fool

Feel my sexy groove

Well I'm gonna have a lemon drop, go home take a

snooze

Whoa hold on a second sister, that's right I'm

digging you

Your smiles, your kisses, and that's right, your tata

too

But your eyes bleed with lust, coveting your lonely

soul

I have to break it to you, something you need to

know,

Your beauty's just an illusion, which always fades

with time

Just like the Benz you drove you, you didn't see the

stop it sign

I revert back to my mama I recall she used to say

Don't worship the mighty dollar from only paper it
is made

True ecstasy lies beyond your ego let it go and you
will see

All God's faithful dreams awaiting you and me

So watch the fish hooks girl as they reach out to pull
you in

You'll lose everybody no one will be your true
friend

Desire's a great thing a spark of intelligence

But don't go lose your mind and all your common
sense

Get an education, knock it out, earn a degree,

And remember what mama said,

It's not always about me, me, me

Chapter 13 - Faces and Heels

"Blood, sweat and respect. The first two you give.
The last you earn. Give it. Earn it."

The Rock

The more you learn about what it means to be an actor and performer, the more you come to realize that life itself is like playing out a very long and dramatic role. Sometimes, though, no amount of training and studying can prepare you for the roles that life throws at you. You have to be able to roll with the punches and adapt yourself to new situations. It's like doing an improv show; you have to think on your feet and quickly figure out how to respond.

These thoughts and feelings came into my mind when I suddenly had the opportunity to try out pro wrestling! I certainly never saw myself as a pro wrestler. Back in the 80's, they always looked like they were pumped up on steroids, wore hilarious outfits, and had crazy gimmicks… it was like a big cartoon. I never really got into it because I always thought it was too over the top. I did, however, respect the athletes involved, and I knew that wrestling had a huge audience. I was always impressed by how much people loved it.

One day, I got a call from a former WWE pro wrestler named Jimmy "Wang" Yang. He told me he'd been a fan of *The Last Dragon* his entire life and that he'd been using the soundtrack as his opening theme when he came out to the ring before a match. Jimmy asked me to do a few wrestling shows with him. It was completely unexpected and I had never thought about doing something like this before, but I've always liked physical challenges and knew this would be an interesting experience.

Jimmy lived in Ohio, so he flew out to New York to meet me at my gym. He was a nice and easy-going guy, . I was surprised to notice that he wasn't very big at all, maybe around 5'8" and 180 lbs. or so (he said that wrestling had changed a bit and you no longer needed to be so big). He explained that he wanted to do some team matches with me. We were to train for a week in Ohio and then we'd enter a match or two. Jimmy assured me that I would do fine and that with my skills I would pick it up quickly. He was pretty convincing, so I decided to go for it!

I went out to Ohio and Jimmy began to teach me some wrestling maneuvers. I'd been a martial artist most of my life, but these moves were really different and presented a unique challenge. At the same time, I learned quickly. Jimmy brought some young wrestlers in to move around with me. They threw each other around the ropes, all over the ring, and pretty much anywhere they could. It was pretty wild, but I didn't feel quite comfortable with the whole process. I let them know how I felt and they respected my wishes. I think that some of the weirdness came from the notion that a person that I just met was going to grab me, pick me up, and throw me around. It felt awkward! I never got completely used to it during our week of training.

Jimmy said that our match was set for the following week in Kentucky and we eventually drove out to the event. It was a real small town and I didn't know what to expect. We went inside the event building and let's just say that it wasn't the highest quality joint. It was basically an event hall where tables and chairs were placed around the room. There was also a bar in the corner of the room, complete with a popcorn maker. It was a real jacked up place! Jimmy went to inspect the ring. He reported back that the ring seemed to be somewhat unsteady, firm in some areas and soft in others. The promoters promised to work on it, so that by the time we came out to wrestle, it would be in better shape. Jimmy didn't seem too concerned about it, so I just followed his lead. I trusted that he was a pro and knew how things worked in the pro wrestling world.

We went backstage and there were a lot of other wrestlers, putting on their outfits and warming up. They were really into it and it was an interesting scene. It seemed like everyone was just acting like kids in Halloween costumes, kind of like they were on a playground. The wrestlers were mostly young nice guys in their 20's, but some were older and looked a bit burnt out. I guess it was the wear and tear of being banged up in matches and the fact that they didn't make much money with it. If you wanted real success, you had to make it to the big show, and get a good contract with WWE. There were very few wrestlers who had actually made it that far, and most of these guys were just hustling and trying to get what they could. It definitely reminded me of the movie industry.

After a while the show started. Jimmy and I were going to be in the seventh match of the evening. While we waited our turn, I warmed up and watched the other matches. I was fascinated with how the wrestlers around me were all practicing their moves without hurting each other. They made it look so concise and simple. When they were in the ring, though, they performed an elaborate show, and the moves looked so explosive, elaborate and dangerous. They finally called us to come out. I was a little excited and thought to myself, "Alright, here we go…my first pro wrestling match!"

We went out into the main arena and people were yelling different things. The audience was just wild and eating it all up, it was pretty funny. In pro wrestling terms, Jimmy and I were called "faces", which meant that we were the good guys. The opponents, or the bad guys, were called "heels". The people in the audience started to recognize me, and I could hear them loudly chatting to each other, "Oh my God…is that Bruce Leroy?" To tell you the truth, I was embarrassed. I didn't know what to feel. It was very different from doing professional theater on a stage somewhere, playing a serious role. Was I supposed to be playing Bruce Leroy? Or was I just supposed to be myself? It was very awkward and it got worse.

When I stepped into the ring, I realized that the ring was in exactly the same poor condition as before… they hadn't changed anything at all! It was dipping and sliding, and it felt like we were walking on a waterbed or some cheap mattress. But we couldn't stop now. The show must go on, right? I was doing jump kicks and back somersaults, and I was afraid I was going to break my neck and die. The ring felt so unstable and I was nervous throughout the whole routine. But in the end, the crowd loved it. I walked out of there taking a breath of relief, trying to get my head back together after an extremely awkward experience. I was beginning to have second thoughts about this whole thing, but Jimmy persuaded me to relax. He said it was my first show and that he'd double check the ring before we went out to the next venue.

Our next match was in Ohio and we began rehearsing right away. Our opponents were two short Irish twins who had a sort of leprechaun gimmick. They had some local popularity and I thought they were pretty cool guys. The twins had some different ideas that they wanted to try out in the match, but Jimmy overruled them and insisted that they perform the choreography his way. Jimmy had done the big show, the WWE, and it seemed like he had seniority over a lot of the other wrestlers who we encountered. He made sure that others knew who he was, his experience, and that they gave him the right kind of respect. I was new to this game and didn't interfere at all. I wasn't used to this style because when I rehearse with other actors, we all try to behave like we're equals, with no seniority treatment. The pro wrestling world was definitely different in this respect. But Jimmy's ideas and choreography were actually very good. I felt comfortable with them and since I had no experience, I was happy to go along with them. The twins ultimately suppressed their feelings and didn't suggest much else. They were just happy to be in a show with Jimmy and me, and they didn't want to cause a problem.

The match took place in a much bigger venue than the last one. It sat around 600 people, with the ring surrounded by the main floor, as well as a balcony. We all warmed up with the other wrestlers and waited for our turn. This time I felt like I was well rehearsed and the ring was perfect, so I expected things to go much more smoothly.

Boy, was I wrong! One thing about doing live work is that just about anything can go wrong and many things won't work out as originally planned. This can actually be a gift; when something goes wrong, it can create a raw moment that feels true and unscripted, and it can draw the audience even more. If scenes are over rehearsed, they lose the illusion of reality that we're trying to achieve on stage and things can become too predictable. This definitely wasn't one of those times!

At first, it seemed like everything was going great. I was going through my routine with one of the twins and Jimmy was fighting with the other one. But when I looked over at Jimmy and his opponent, it seemed more like a real fight, like they weren't going that easy on each other. I kept my cool but it seemed strange. All of a sudden, I saw Jimmy slam his opponent up against one of the barricades that separated the audience from us. It looked pretty rough! After that, I saw his opponent come back with a palm right up to Jimmy's nose. I continued to fight my twin but things were going a bit haywire. When I turned around next, Jimmy came crawling into the ring with blood streaming out of his nose. I thought to myself, was this something I wasn't privy to? Was this supposed to happen? Was this fake blood? But no, it was real blood! Jimmy sprawled himself out in the middle of the ring, lying on the mat. He was pretending to be in pain, but with real blood spewing out of his nose, he didn't have to act too much.

The whole scene totally threw me off and I lost my place in the choreography. The twins noticed that I was out of place, so they grabbed my forearms and quickly whispered, "Taimak, just go with it." I went along with their plan, and they picked me up over their shoulders. I felt like I was at a Six Flags amusement park on a rollercoaster. They slammed me right onto my back. Thank God for my martial arts experience! I understood how to slap out and take the fall, which meant that I had to tuck my chin into my chest and roll with the motion. I was fine, and when I got up, I saw my chance to perform the finishing move that we had rehearsed. It was a flying sidekick to the upper back of one of the twins. He was turned around, pretending to look for Jimmy and his brother, and I was supposed to take advantage of his vulnerability. I pulled off the final move. Jimmy and I then celebrated the victory. The audience loved it!

In the end, pro wrestling wasn't my calling in life, but it was an interesting and really unique experience. The fans were so loud and energetic, and I just fed off of their energy. It felt great to be around so many people who were cheering out my name, especially when they recognized me and were so excited to see Bruce Leroy in person. When I got over my embarrassment about being a wrestler, I was honored to perform in front of all of these people.

Not long after, I decided to find a new way to change things up and get some fresh exposure for my career. I chose to direct a short film. I could show my ability to write and direct, and I would also be able showcase all of the good actors I knew. I wanted to help my friends prove their talent to the world. I cast two guys I knew for the short film: one was an independent professional wrestler who was great at making the audience laugh while putting them down in a funny way, while the other was a painter and actor who loved to get high and who also had a strange and humorously harmless temper. They both had interesting and comical personalities and I knew they would enjoy the attention of being in a short film.

I chose to base the story on my painter friend's life – he was a unique and original cat, and I felt that people would be fascinated to find out more about him. Eventually, this short film project turned into two shorts. I kept my original idea about the life of my painter friend, but I also started to write another story about a group of go-go dancers. I thought the latter would be visually appealing and I wanted to focus on a few different girls and their interactions with one another. I knew a few dancers as well as a bunch of women who were looking to try their hand at acting that would be great in these roles.

As I wrote these two stories, many of my friends in the business urged me to put myself in these films. Their logic was that people already knew who I was, while the others actors were all unknown. If I was in the films themselves, the more attention the film would receive, allowing for greater exposure at film festivals. They also pointed out that it would help my acting as well. I understood their point, so I brainstormed a way to combine both of these short films into one story where I would also have a role. I changed the go-go dancers into women who worked at a fetish club, and the story was changed into a provocative murder mystery called *I've Seen Things*. I would play a detective who is tasked with investigating a murderer who frequented the fetish club. The murderer would be a wealthy and powerful art gallery owner, and my painter friend would play the murderer's bitter and vengeful assistant. Finally, my pro wrestler friend would play an African prince who gets caught up in all of this intrigue.

I had enough to get me started, so I began to look for other actors and cameramen to shoot it. I also did a Kickstarter campaign and raised $5,000, which wasn't a lot considering the undertaking. I had no idea what I was getting into. It was the first film I ever produced, wrote, directed, and starred in, and I didn't even have an assistant. What was I going to do? Luckily, I met a new friend who helped take some of this difficulty off of my shoulders. His name was Nikwan Murphy and he was priceless! He was a cop and a weapons specialist, and he answered all of my questions about police work. He gave me the information that I needed about certain firearms and he helped me to track down the filming locations that I was looking for. In addition, he was a martial artist, who knew a lot of the same people that I did from the old days. I asked him to be involved in the film – it was a no-brainer, because he had so much experience and so much great advice. I also met two cameramen – Bob Scott and Brandon Herman – who wanted to work with me. I enlisted them to shoot the film, and we were set! These guys had experience, they were trustworthy, they always showed up on time, and they had excellent ideas. What could go wrong, right?

Unfortunately, I had to let go of both my painter and pro wrestler friends. After we shot the first scene, they both refused to sign the release forms. If they didn't sign the forms, I wouldn't be able to use them in the movie. Basically, they were going on a power trip and holding the film hostage. They were thinking that this might turn into something big and they wanted to make a lot of money with it. It wouldn't have been a problem if they were forthcoming in the beginning with their expectations. But they knew from the start that this was purely voluntary, and there wasn't going to be any form of payment. It was meant to be a workshop. Maybe something good would come out of it, but it was more about exposure and gaining experience and having a good time. However, when they showed up to the set and saw all of the actors and professional cameramen, and all the excitement that comes with making a movie, the whole thing started to look much bigger than they had expected. They thought that this would be a payday for them. I guess sometimes, people become legends in their own minds. You give them a little attention, and they go way overboard.

I fired both of them and hired other actors. You should never let two bad apples ruin the pie. I shot a bunch of scenes and did a lot of work on the project, and it was looking good. I eventually spoke with a friend of mine who was an independent filmmaker, and he persuaded me to write a full-length version of the story. I stopped shooting the short so that I could reassess and get a better look at the project. I don't regret stopping, even though there were some solid scenes and it looked great. I just needed some time to think about how I could make the necessary changes to transform the film into a full cinematic experience.

Joel Eisenberg, another one of my writer/filmmaker friends, thought that I should bring my ideas out to the American Film Institute (AFI) market in Los Angeles, where filmmakers from all over the world try to make deals and sell their films. I knew other actors and filmmakers who were always going to AFI, but I had never been there myself. I thought that all I needed to get my movie made was a talented actor (I was naïve, just like Bruce Leroy). I didn't know anything about that side of things! I had to find a production company that would recognize the potential in my story. While I looked for financing for the film, I started working on another feature screenplay called *The Professor*.

While I was reassessing my short film and doing other similar projects, something special was happening with *The Last Dragon*. The film was being rediscovered by a whole new generation of fans. People who grew up with the movie were showing it to their kids, it was being referenced in songs and pop culture, and retrospective screenings of the film were selling out at specialty theaters all over the country. I didn't know it yet, but I was soon going to get the chance to interact with countless fans of *The Last Dragon*, which would lead into one of the most magical and humbling stages of my life.

Chapter 14 - The Return of the Dragon

"What lies behind us and what lies before us are tiny matters compared to what lies within us."

Ralph Waldo Emerson

In early 2014, I received a call from a guy named Demetrius Angelo. He wanted to put on an event called The Urban Action Showcase and Expo, where he would screen cult action movies and shine a spotlight on old school action stars. Demetrius felt that I would be a perfect fit for this event and he told me that *The Last Dragon* was exactly the sort of film that he had in mind when he created the event. I was interested in his offer but I didn't know much about Demetrius at first. I'll be honest, I had gotten cynical over the years about invitations. You never really know what someone will want or how they might try to exploit you. Ron Van Clief said that Demetrius really wanted to honor me for my contributions to martial arts film and to black culture.

When I finally spoke with Demetrius, I immediately realized that he was a gentleman and a honorable person with a unique sense of vision. He told me that I was an inspiration to him as a martial artist and as a person (hey, flattery will get you every time), and he seemed really genuine about everything he was saying. He revealed that we had actually met when he was 16. I made an appearance at a great martial arts event known as the US Capitol Classics, it's produced by long time kung fu practitioner Dennis Brown and Demetrius was there for a competitive tournament. Demetrius remembered that I was kind to him and that I told him to never stop training. It sure sounded like something I would say! The meeting really had a big effect on him, because he was a huge fan of *The Last Dragon*. I could tell that the martial arts culture really flowed through his blood, and he was passionate about the whole thing. I decided that he deserved my support and I was excited about the opportunity.

This would be the first event that Demetrius ever put on, and he was trying to do something big and ambitious right from the start. His ultimate goal with The Urban Action Showcase and Expo was to celebrate African Americans, Asians, Latinos, women, and other minorities in the independent action film genre. He wanted to honor me, Ron Van Clief, Kelly Hu, Michael Jai White, Fred "The Hammer" Williamson, and indie ilm writer Ben Ramsey. I was honored to be included with them.

The event took place at the Hilton on 6th Avenue in New York City. I showed up to the event in the morning and walked into one of the big conference rooms where everyone was setting up tables and preparing for the fans to arrive. I would be sitting at the tables with the other celebrities and comic book artists who would be selling their work, and we would all sign autographs and meet the fans. As the day went on, we waited for the fans to show up, and it was a little slow at first. That was okay, though. We were all in good spirits and very supportive. We all knew that it takes time for things to develop. After all, this was the first time that this event had ever been put on.

I got the chance to meet the other celebrities, who were all interesting people. The Hammer still carried the same sense of humor, charisma, and attitude that he was so famous for. He had me in stitches the entire time. After the autograph signing and the comic book sale ended, an award ceremony took place later that evening. The whole event had a lot of heart and you could tell that it was going to grow into something special. When the event was over, we were all impressed with the way that Demetrius had managed the whole affair. We knew that Demetrius had some work to do so that he could get the event to the kind of level that he was aspiring to, but that would just take time and more experience.

I spoke to Demetrius the following week and he told me that he wanted to throw a party in celebration of the 30th anniversary of *The Last Dragon*. Yes, it had already been 30 years since those cameras began rolling back in 1984! I thought that it was a great idea and I agreed. Demetrius contacted Sony Pictures and asked them if they would be interested in showing up in some way to support the event. They were very diplomatic, and while they did make themselves available, they passed on sponsoring the event. We were on our own, but I knew that it would be a great event. We would put on a big screening of the movie, and Craig Sutton (a fan for life who runs the legendary *Last Dragon* fan site) would MC the Q&A after the film. I was excited and I could tell that the fans were really interested and hyped up. It was going to be great!

We did the event in November and it was really something exceptional. It was a packed house and a really fun time. We got a bunch of cast members from the film to make an appearance: Christopher Murney, who played Eddie Arcadian, members of Sho's gang, Henry and Mike, who were the two Chinese cats, and Ron Van Clief, who did some fight choreography for the film, all showed up. It was a pretty emotional feeling to be there with so many fans and the people who worked on the movie with me, talking about and the project that held such a special place in my heart for so many years. I truly wish that Denise, Julius and Leo had been there to experience it with all of us.

From the beginning, from the auditions, we knew "The Last Dragon" was going to be a hoot. For me, as an Asian-American actor, this was an opportunity to work on a comedy, which I love doing, to play "jive talking soul brothers," which played against type, and to say all my prepositions, which precluded any Chinese accented pidgin-ny phrasing.

Oddly, even though we weren't asked during auditions to use a Chinese accent, we spent our first day on the set shooting the scenes using accents. The scenes were not funny this way. The next day we re-shot all the scenes, I believe at the insistence of Mr. Gordy, "jive talking" without the Chinese accents. Now this was funny. We had great fun with this and enjoyed it tremendously.

We also enjoyed working with Taimak who was young and inexperienced, but was personable and eager. His natural charm was an asset. His physical and martial arts skills were impressive as well.

We had no idea that this movie would become the cult classic it is. To this day Mike Chin and I get recognized by fans of "The Last Dragon" and some of these encounters are pretty hilarious, too.

I continue to ply my trade in film, tv and stage.

Henry Lui

This screening was just one of the first steps in what would soon become a huge revival of *The Last Dragon*. Around this time, I started doing comic book convention appearances. While I was at a comic con in San Antonio, I met an actor and martial artist named Steve Cardenas, who played one of the Red Rangers on the cult classic *Power Rangers* show. Steve introduced himself and told me that he was a fan of *The Last Dragon*. We became friendly and he introduced me to staff members from a company called IDDS Management. The people at IDDS felt they could help me to appear at more conventions and screening events, and I was happy to team up with them. I worked closely with Daniel Louzau from IDDS, who had the idea to approach the popular Drafthouse movie theater chain in Texas to do a 30th anniversary tour for *The Last Dragon*. We would travel all over the state, screening the film, doing Q&A sessions and meet-and-greet events for the fans. The Drafthouse theaters were very interested in the idea, and they wanted us to start the tour at their flagship theater in Austin.

There are moments in your life that you'll never forget...and this tour was definitely one of them. I posted the details on my social media pages and got a lot of great feedback from fans who were so excited that I was coming to Texas. At first, Daniel wasn't so sure that the tour would be that successful. He didn't quite realize the level of fan interest and dedication that we were dealing with; this was his first time working with me and he didn't know that much about the fanbase of *The Last Dragon*. He knew that it was a beloved film and a cult classic, but it was from 30 years ago. It was underrated and it was never given the media attention that other films in the genre were given throughout the years, like *The Karate Kid* or the *Blade* series. He never directly came out and said it, but I could sense his concern about the theaters not being able to sell out the seats. He didn't realize the impact the movie made on people just about everywhere! I reassured him and his other staff members that there was really nothing to worry about. I confidently told them: "You'll see…these fans are something else!" In the end, I was right!

> *Without a doubt, "The Last Dragon" was one of the most enjoyable film projects that I was ever involved with. We (Henry, Fred and I) had a blast. I knew then that I would never play a role like this, again. That inspired me to go all out and have fun.*
>
> *When I first met Tai, he was quiet, intense and very intimidating. I didn't talk much to him on set as he*

236

was very focused. I remember the scene when he literally kicked down the fortune cookie factory door. They had rigged the door so that it would swing open when kicked. But Tai still had to give it a good kick. He kicked it so hard that it flew into me and slammed my shoulder. You can see it in the scene. Then to make matters even worse Tai grabs me and slams me against the wall. Michael Shultz didn't help matters. He kept yelling: "Jack him up". It was pretty intense. The fear on my face was real. Then when they yelled "Cut". Tai gave me a big smile. I knew then that we would get along.

After the film was released I couldn't walk the streets of New York without someone recognizing me. It was pretty cool and still is to this day.

Right now I am still acting. However, my focus is more on teaching stage combat on the college level, fight choreography and the occasional stunt gig. I am a Fight Master with The Society of American Fight Directors. I keep in touch with Henry and Tai. Life is good."

Michael Chin

I received an email from Daniel about two weeks before the tour started. He said excitedly, "Austin is sold out! Would you be open to doing two screenings?" I didn't have to think twice - of course,

I agreed. I knew that they would be able to pack the theater, but even I didn't expect the demand to be so strong. A week before I was about to leave, Houston was also sold out and they added two extra screenings there. Dallas and San Antonio sold out as well, and it was now a sold out tour! Saira, one of the staff, who now owns her own booking company called Idolwerks called me up and said, "We'd better get more DVDs to sign. We're not going to have enough!" I was completely pumped about the whole thing. When it was time to fly to Texas, I left for the airport with so much momentum and energy in my body. I could sense that I was about to have a special experience. I told myself, "Let's go! This is it!"

The flagship theater in Austin was huge (they do things big in Texas!) and I was really impressed. If I lived in the area, it's definitely a place I would enjoy going to. I almost felt like I was at Universal Studios. Just being in that theater was an event in its own right. The lobby was incredibly spacious and filled with little attractions. They had a full bar, a dance floor, as well as booths where you could have dinner. They even had a karaoke room! The people behind the Drafthouse knew that audiences don't want to come to the movies to sit on plastic seats and eat plastic popcorn – that sort of experience was best left behind in those old grindhouse theaters on 42nd Street. I mean, this place really was a theme park for movie buffs. I met the very cool theater manager - he told me that he was a huge fan and that *The Last Dragon* inspired him to train in martial arts - and he showed us around before we set up the signing table. I had DVDs, shirts, and photos for the fans. I was so excited to connect with all of the people who were going to come out. My fans are amazing and show me so much love. It's a great feeling, because no matter who they are in their regular life, they completely turn into a kid when they meet me. I love it and I just have so much appreciation for them.

The screening's moderator was Craig MacLennan. He was a comedian and a big fan of the film. I don't know if it was Drafthouse's intention, but the staff really knew *The Last Dragon* well and were serious fans. It made me feel really comfortable, and I was right in my element. While the staff waited for people to get to their seats, they played fun clips from martial arts films, clips of me that they found on YouTube, and other fun and appropriately themed clips. After about ten minutes of that, they introduced me to the audience. I entered the theater and I could immediately feel buzz in the room…everyone was screaming, it was truly amazing. People were hollering out, "Leeeeerooooy!" It was a trip! Craig made a few opening jokes and he did a great job of moderating things. He kept everyone laughing and we worked off each other quite nicely. He kept cracking jokes and he fed me some lines, saying things like, "Taimak, how do you look so young? I want to drink your blood!" I laughed and responded: "Martial arts, living a healthy and balanced lifestyle and keeping good people in your life."

After I joked around with Craig for a few minutes and the crowd was really pumped up, I turned to the audience and just said a few words, "Hello everyone, it's a complete pleasure to be in Austin, Texas with y'all. I've had a 30 year romance with this movie and all of you fans, and I'm honored that you still love this film as if it came out today. Please enjoy the movie and I'll be back later for the Q&A." The crowd applauded and cheered, and I left so that the movie could

Posing in front of Tribeca Cinemas during the 30th anniversary celebration, 2015.
Photo by Federoff Colin

start. I eventually went back into the theater to watch some of the film with the audience. I really liked the sensation of being there with the audience, just tapping into the positive vibes in the room. I love hearing the things that come out of people's mouths as they watch the movie. They cheer, sing along to the songs, repeat the lines, and even stand up in their seats and do martial arts moves. It's always like being at a wild and passionate, family party. It's a magical feeling. After the screening, the Q&A went really well. Most of the time, fans tend to ask me the same questions that I've heard many times before, but it never bothers me. I'm grateful and I just love interacting with them and making them smile.

At the second screening in Austin, I had a few other fun surprises. I was approached by a gentleman who owns a juice company. He came over and gave me a bottled drink that contained orange juice and Turmeric root. I was pleasantly surprised when I saw the label – the drink was called "The Glow" and it was inspired by *The Last Dragon*! It still blows my mind that this film has had such a big impact on so many people. It will always be an honor to meet these fans…I know that it brightens up their day to get a chance to meet me, but I hope they know that it brightens up my day when I get to meet them. I also met another fan at this screening: Elijah Wood and his brother came to the show, and Craig introduced me to him after the Q&A. Elijah told me that he was a fan of the film and that he wanted to meet me in person. I sat down with Elijah, his brother, Craig, and a couple of other people after the screening – it was a memorable night.

Every city on the tour had a magic moment that I'll never forget. In San Antonio, there was a sense of passion and heart that refused to be denied. Daniel told me that San Antonio had quite a large number of low income residents. To me, it's a blessing to be able to meet and connect with people who are struggling. There so many people who are diamonds in the rough. I hope that I'm able to inspire them – I definitely know that they inspire me, each and every day. At the screening, I met a young girl in her early 20's. She was Latina with black-framed glasses and such a cute face, and she brought all her Taimak memorabilia with her. She was so nervous that she couldn't speak. She gave me a hug and her body was shaking like a leaf the entire time. She ran away as quickly as she could and went into the theater to sit down. I was really touched!

When we held the screening in Dallas, we were treated to a special appearance by actor and martial arts star Ernie Reyes Jr. He had recently moved to Richardson, right outside of Dallas, and fans were elated that he came out to meet them and celebrate the movie with all of us. Ernie actually had a small part in *The Last Dragon* – his dad was a choreographer on the film and it was his first exposure in the movie business. Ernie gave me a lot of respect and he told the audience how *The Last Dragon* was his first film and that I had inspired him ever since he was a little kid. I hung out with Ernie during the screening and we watched the movie with his little girl. She really loved it! After the screening ended, we had some fun during the Q&A, breaking a few boards, karate style. It was just an amazing time.

We finished the Dallas screening and packed up for Houston, the last city on the tour. The Houston fans were fun. There was a guy who was pissed that Denise didn't come out. I told him that everyone had reached out to her but she wasn't interested in doing the tour. I jokingly suggested to him, "She has a Facebook profile man, go see what you can do." When the last screening was over, I asked people to take a vow of non-violence when it came to their words, thoughts, and actions. I originally got the idea from Dr. Deepak Chopra; it made a major difference in my life, and it really elevated me as a person. This sort of non-violent thinking disciplined my thoughts and forced me to look for alternative means of dealing with hostile situations. Some people took the vow and others didn't, but most people were into it and were willing to give it a shot. I told everyone, "Hey, if you break the vow, you can always say sorry and put it back together again."

The whole tour event was simply extraordinary. I felt so much love from so many fans. It's hard to find the words to explain how I felt... being there, after 30 long years, was simply magical. I met so many wonderful people, of all ages, genders and races, and I felt such a great connection with all of them. I was so touched by the love that I even shed a few tears of joy. I really enjoy every event where I have the opportunity to interact with fans and reach out to people. It's been a huge honor to be the star of such a magical film that has touched so many lives. Whenever I make an appearance at screenings and comic book conventions, it's another chance to get the word out about the unique experience of *The Last Dragon* and the big effect that it's had on people. There are times when people don't realize that I'm at these conventions, either because they didn't check the website or my appearance wasn't promoted very well. It would be different if I was as popular as the Kardashians and had a million Instagram followers. I'm working on it.

In the meantime, I'm simply honored by all of the people I've met at these events. I've had parents bring their kids to visit me at events that are miles away from their hometown. One gentleman told me that he came all the way from Canada. His 6 year-old daughter actually watches *The Last Dragon* every day! When she came over to my table, she had a full karate gi on – she was absolutely adorable. I've even had two separate couples tell me that it wasn't for *The Last Dragon*, they never would have gotten married. They tell me things like, "The film connected us. We saw the movie when we first started dating, we laughed and cried, and we kept watching it. The film brought us closer and closer together, and we love to repeat the lines to each other. There was a time when we watched the movie just about every other day!" It's so humbling to hear things like this. When I'm at these conventions, I sometimes sit back in my seat and just think about how thankful I am to be where I'm at in my life.

People ask me if I get sick of these screenings and convention gigs, dealing with the same movie over and over. I tell them, "It's funny, but I don't. Just try to imagine the feeling that everywhere you go, people want to hug you and give you love." Yes, it can be overwhelming at times, but that's why I show up to these things – to be overwhelmed with these great encounters. It definitely takes energy and it can be exhausting, and I'm happy to do it and to continue to be a part of something special. It's an absolute honor to answer questions from all of my fans and to sense their passion and energy.

There are so many films made every year, and 30 years from now, most of them will be forgotten. To play the lead role in a movie that has touched so many people and inspired so many athletes, even after 30 years really feels great. I want to make more movies that inspire people - I truly enjoy acting in every context, on the stage, on television, and in film, and I have so much more to share with people. I'm grateful, however, that I had this opportunity to be in

The Last Dragon and to make an impact on so many people. When I think back on this film, it was unforgettable experience. To be able to work with so many talented people in one movie, to work hands-on with Motown legend Berry Gordy and director Michael Schultz, to make an impact on all of these fans, to even shoot the movie in the neighborhoods that I grew up in around New York City...in a word, it was extraordinary. I was depressed as a child, full of love, but pain was all around me. I dreamt of being a superhero just like Bruce Lee - the fact that I was cast in a film where my character, like myself, idolized Bruce, was simply a miracle.

My hope is that everybody has the opportunity to do an extraordinary thing that they'll never forget. I know that you can do it. One way for you to believe that you are an extraordinary person, is to take mental notes of all the acknowledgments that you receive from others. You can even write them down in a journal or make a collage of pictures that express the different ways that other people see you as an extraordinary person.

I know there are self-doubts. It's like we've been programmed to think badly of ourselves because we aren't perfect. I read that Bruce Lee would write down all of his negative thoughts about himself on a piece of paper, light a match to it and watch it burn. Remind yourself that you are someone who other people love. Go through life with confidence and feel proud of who you are. You don't have to pump your chest out when you walk down the street. You just have to know that you're the guy or gal who can get the job. Who can start your own business. Who can be a great mom or dad. Who has the humility to learn and listen to others. The key is just to remember, each and every day, that you are special. Walk with your head up, even in darkness...because you know who you are.

Chapter 15 – Looking to the Future

"The brave men did not kill dragons. The brave men rode them."

George R. R. Martin

In the past few years, I've had the good fortune to be involved in a number of wonderful projects. The universe is funny like that – you don't get anything that you want for a long time, and then all of sudden you get tons of opportunities at once. I'm grateful that I'm able to move into the future with so many chances to do great things.

One of these opportunities was born back in 2009, when I met a young actor and martial artist named Alexander Wraith. He told me that he was a big fan of *The Last Dragon* and he wanted to get to know me. He was a solid athlete with a good work ethic and had a great sense of humor. I liked him, so we hung out a few times and worked out together. Alex was highly motivated to make a martial arts comedy film and he knew a lot of people in the movie business that could help him to make it happen. He called me up one day and told me that he wanted me to meet his friend and screenwriting partner, Sean Stone (the son of director Oliver Stone). Sean and Alex were developing a martial arts comedy project called *Enter the Fist* and they wanted me to be in it.

They told me they were eagerly looking for financing for the film and that they wanted me to play a character named Dragon. The role was a tribute to my performance in *The Last Dragon*. In fact, the whole movie would be filled with throwback references and jokes about classic martial arts movies. I thought it was a ridiculous idea, but hey, it's a comedy, right? I liked these guys and I was willing to give them a chance. I told them that I appreciated the offer and that they should let me know when they had some financial details really locked down.

Five years went by and I was busy with the 30th anniversary celebration of *The Last Dragon*, making appearances at screenings and conventions around the country. Suddenly, Alex called me out of the blue and said "Come on Dragon, we've got some money and we're shooting!" Alex can be a bold and demanding guy, though not in a bad way – he comes on strong and he really draws you in with his enthusiasm. I said to him, "Whoa, okay, slow down! You've got to give me the dates first, my brother." It just so happened that I had two free weeks at exactly the time that they needed me to shoot my scenes. It worked out perfectly! I wanted a second opinion on the script, so I asked my friend Joel to give it a read. He read the script and he thought it was just too ridiculous and wasn't too into it. I understood where he was coming from, but I knew that while at times stories can seem really silly on paper, they take on a life of their own when talented actors perform those lines and interact with each other. When you're making a comedy, the real value of what you're doing is going to come across in the performance and not so much on the page of a script. I thought there was enough in this script that we could make something fun. At the very least, college kids would think it was a blast.

I worked out the contract with Alex and Sean, and they flew me out to Los Angeles to start shooting. They booked some pretty interesting and diverse talent: Danny Trejo, Tiny Lister, Ernie Reyes Jr., as well as former UFC champion Don Frye, tough guy Chuck Zitto (infamously known as the guy who roughed up Jean Claude Van Damme), Jean Claude Van Damme's daughter Bianca, and many others. I would get to do an extended fight scene with WWE star Bill Goldberg, as well as a short fight scene with Simon Rhee from *Best of the Best*. I could tell that this was going to be a lot of fun!

I had one big concern, though. I was dealing with a groin injury and it was going to need a few more months to heal. It was an injury that was destined to happen after all my years of training. It's a common occurrence among athletes who work with their legs, like karate experts, ballerinas, runners, and football players. I've really given my legs a serious workout over the years. I also can't help going overboard when I'm training by doing tons of high kicks through the air. I simply love the feeling of soaring through the air and kicking as high as I can, nailing the training bag with a well-aimed thwack. It's an amazing sensation!

The groin injury happened back in 2011 when I was training at Marcelo Garcia's Academy in Manhattan. Marcelo was the World Brazilian Jiu-Jitsu Champion and became known for winning an impressive match against the great fighter Renzo Grazie at a tournament when he was 19. People in the Brazilian Jiu-Jitsu community were all talking about this young guy. He was one of the challengers to beat, a young champion that wasn't doing old style, closed guard Brazilian Jiu-Jitsu. He revolutionized and popularized an open guard style, using a technique called the "X-Guard". I wanted to start practicing Brazilian Jiu-Jitsu again, and Marcelo seemed like the perfect person to meet.

When I showed up at the Academy, it was crowded. It was summer and everyone was drenched in sweat. I met Marcelo and we hit it off immediately. Many people there recognized me and they told Marcelo how much they loved *The Last Dragon*. Marcelo had never seen the movie, but later found out that his best friend in Brazil was also a huge fan of the film. Marcelo felt a little out of the loop, like something epic and amazing had been happening right behind his back, without him knowing it. He has an amiable personality and he was just really easy to get along with. He is very focused on making his style of Brazilian Jiu-Jitsu into a world-famous style, and he's definitely succeeding. It's becoming more and more common for me to hear, "Wow, you trained in Brazilian Jiu-Jitsu with Marcelo Garcia? He's the best!" There are certainly other practitioners who are equally as good and who have great skills in their own right, but Marcelo is definitely in the top echelon of Brazilian Jiu-Jitsu fighters in the world.

About a year and a half into my training, I felt a pain in my groin area while I was rolling ("rolling" is the term for sparring in Brazilian Jiu-Jitsu). I went home and rested up, but although my groin was still sore, I still came back to train the next day. I began to roll and was warmed up. Training with injuries is just a part of practicing martial arts. This groin injury started to nag at me, though, and I couldn't walk around without limping. I realized that I had pulled my groin pretty badly and had to stop rolling. I just mellowed out for about a couple weeks. Unfortunately, it eventually got to the point where I couldn't roll at all, because I didn't have enough strength and there was too much pain in my left leg. I had pulled my groin before and it generally takes about 6 months for this type of injury to heal, so I decided to rest and wait it out.

Around 8 months went by, but I still felt some pain in my groin. However, the pain was greatly reduced. I waited a few more months and while the groin wasn't feeling too bad, I noticed that the side of my hip was now aching as well. That's when I decided that I needed to do something right away. I had an MRI and they saw that there was a tear in my labrum. The labrum is cartilage that lays over the ball in your hip joint. It's a very difficult injury to heal, because very little blood frequents that area. Blood flow is the source of healing muscle, tendon and ligament tears. Although my tear didn't go all the way across and it wasn't that bad, it did cause discomfort and occasional pain. The doctor said that it would heal over time, but it was going to be tough.

It had already been a year, so I decided to add massages and to eat a more anti-inflammatory style of diet. Although that helped a bit, it didn't get rid of the pain. The whole situation left me frustrated. I was unable to train at the level of intensity that I normally love to maintain. I wasn't able to do any kicks, so I was getting quite depressed. The young lady who I was dating at the time did her best to help me get over it and she really felt for me, but my injury made me cranky and it created tension between us. I was aware of my issue so I talked to her and we worked it out. I tried to wait and let the injury heal for a few more months, but I eventually came to the conclusion that I had to do something drastic. I knew I didn't want to be cut and opened up in surgery, though.

Fortunately, I had become friendly with one of Marcelo's black belts, a former UFC fighter named Kurt Pellegrino. He recommended a treatment that he'd gone through after experiencing horrible tendon and muscle tears in his groin. It was called platelet-rich plasma therapy, and it involves taking your blood, processing it to concentrate the platelets, and injecting the concentrate into the injured part of your body. The doctor essentially takes the healing properties from your blood (the platelets) and puts them back into your body in the area of your injury. I decided to try this out. I called Kurt's doctor and discussed the situation with him. After viewing my MRI results, he felt my injury was a tough case, due to the nature of the injury. He didn't think the platelet therapy would be sufficient to provide me with a full recovery. He recommended, instead, to do a treatment that would involve stem cells. The basic concept was the same, except they would use bone marrow and fat from my body, a pretty invasive procedure. It was more expensive and not covered by medical insurance. But I did it anyway, and the whole procedure was quite physically unpleasant. Fortunately though, I recovered and felt better. The whole affair was a difficult thing for me to deal with - I had never dealt with an injury that lasted more than six months. I'm grateful that I'm older and more mature, because I was able to work through my frustration and be patient about everything.

This history with my injury made me a bit apprehensive about doing my fight scene with Goldberg in *Enter the Fist*. Goldberg was 6'4 and around 230 lbs., so he was a big dude to be messing with, even if it was just a fake fight! My hip had recovered really well, but my left leg still wasn't that strong and I sometimes felt some pain. Alex was accommodating and he chose to wait until the end of the filming schedule to shoot the fight scene. This would provide a little more time to stretch and take some saunas to prepare, and he promised not to make the fight scene overly long.

When I was finally ready to shoot my scene with Goldberg, I felt good about my injury. I wasn't completely happy about my leg, but I felt pretty confident. I got to the set at 6 PM, because this was going to be an evening shoot. I met Goldberg - he was really nice and we immediately hit it off. He gave me a lot of compliments about my role in *The Last Dragon* and I told him I was equally honored to do a fight scene with him. We rehearsed the fight with the choreographer and we were all happy with how it turned out, so we went back inside into the holding area and waited for our turn to step in front of the camera. If you've ever been on the set of a film, you know that most of time you're sitting around waiting to shoot. The director and cinematographer needs to work with the crew to set up the different scenes, such as proper set-up of the lighting, moving props around, and so on. Around midnight, the production assistant said I should be ready to go in about an hour or so. During this time, Sean Stone, who played the lead, was shooting a fight scene with Michael Dudikoff of *American Ninja* fame, and I figured that would take a good while longer.

I sat down to rest up for a bit and I dozed off. I suddenly woke up when I heard someone shout, "Taimak! They're ready for you!" It was 4 in the morning! I was already exhausted, but hey – the show must go on. It was easy to work with Goldberg and we knew how to handle ourselves in the fight. There were at least twenty people watching our fight scene. As expected, everything went really well. I had to do a spinning kick to Bill's head during this scene and I was a little concerned about it due to my injury. I had to use my stomach muscles to get my leg up, because I didn't want to put too much torque on my injured leg. Alex made me laugh as he directed the scene. He has really good energy and he always wants you to bring a lot of passion to your performance. I really like that about him! Alex is a fan of *The Last Dragon* and a huge fan of Bruce Lee, so he constantly wanted me to do the Bruce Lee scream: "WOOOOWAAAAA!!"

By the time we finished the scene, it was already after 6 in the morning and I just wanted to get out of there and go to bed. The day wasn't over, though. They wanted to shoot an additional scene or two, no fights, just some comedy stuff. By the time we shot the scene, it was well into the morning. We were wrapped for the night and man, I was wrapped too! Everyone was totally beat, but we had got a lot of work done.

After shooting that scene, I was really sore for a week. I spent some time going to the Hare Krishna temple in Culver City - they have a vegetarian buffet there that's absolutely delicious. I also went to an incredibly serene place called the Paramahansa Yogananda center in the Pacific Palisades, right by the beach. I meditated there and just cleared my mind. I later learned that my mother used to take me there as a child, and that instantly made sense to me…it felt like I was in a very familiar and comfortable place. I ultimately decided it was time to focus on getting 100% and healing up to my maximum potential. I didn't have to worry about shooting any physical scenes for a while, so I used the next six months to really put my injury to rest. It's been a very long journey, but I'm almost there. As I'm writing this, it looks like it'll be about three more months. Soon, I'll be able to do a jumping kick just like I was 20 years-old! I'm looking forward to getting back to that level of power and performance.

In addition to my recent film work, I've also had the chance to work with kids in my community, and this has been a really special experience. Angela Crockett is a business owner who works for young people in the Atlantic City community, and she approached me about speaking at different schools in Newark. I began to do a little tour of local schools, giving motivational speeches and inspiring kids to pursue their dreams.

I started off at an elementary school where I was introduced to a large group of 4th and 5th grade kids by their teacher, Ms. Allen. The kids had just recently watched some scenes from *The Last Dragon*, and now they were going to meet the star of the movie! I could tell that the kids were really excited. They had followed up their viewing with a short assignment where they wrote down their dreams for the future, and I was going to talk to them about dreams and achieving your goals.

Ms. Allen introduced me to this class of wonderful kids – there must have been at least 40 or 50 of them in the room. I began with, "You know, when I was your age, I always had a dream of being in a movie, of being an actor, of being an action hero. It was a big, big passion of mine. I told my mother and father that I loved martial arts and that I wanted to be an actor someday..." I told the kids about my dreams of enrolling in the High School of Performing Arts, and I explained to them about my nervousness and fear when I went to audition for the school. My intention was to show the kids that I was human, and that it took work for me to attain my dream of being an actor and a martial artist. The things that I've achieved in my life weren't just given to me – I worked very hard for them. If you have a dream, you have to go out there and get it!

I talked to them some more and then demonstrated a martial arts kata for them, which they really enjoyed. When the kata was over, the kids lined up. One by one, I asked them to tell me what they dreamed to be in the future. I explained to them that the work that they did in school would get them access to that dream. One kid said he wanted to be a UFC fighter. I told him that most MMA fighters start out as amateur athletes and aren't paid anything until they get a big fight in the UFC. In the meantime, they work regular jobs that require some sort of education and they need to balance their professional work life with appearing at tournaments and competitions. I also said that many fighters open up martial arts schools and that this meant they had to understand business, which requires an education. I wanted the kids to see that their dreams didn't just have to be words on the page. There were real, practical ways to go about achieving what they wanted, and it all started with staying in school and studying as hard as they could.

After touring through these schools, I decided to speak to kids at an afterschool program called The Door. I used to go to this program when I was a kid. In the words of the program's creators, The Door was intended to tear down the barriers that prevented young people from succeeding in New York City. The barriers still exist, of course, whether it's the '70s or today, so the program is still in existence. I don't remember how I ended up going to The Door as a kid, but it was a very positive experience for me. When I went there after school, I was able to practice martial arts in a safe environment. The fact that I was able to do that was worth its weight in gold. With that in mind, I knew that The Door was the next place I should go if I wanted to continue to inspire young people. My friend Brenda Torres helped me to work with the programs' management, and we eventually set up a day for me to speak to the kids.

I sat down with about twenty kids and I spoke to them about pursuing their dreams and achieving their goals in the future. Everything was going pretty smoothly as I delivered my seminar to them. Things changed, though, when I asked them to write down their dreams. There was this one kid, probably around 17 years of age, who had a smirk on his face throughout the entire afternoon. He interrupted me and asked me to take a look at what he wrote down on his paper. It said: "I want to rob and fuck people up." I was a little taken aback. It hit me in the heart and I was unexpectedly emotional about it. I realized I had to deal with it calmly and still be committed to this kid so that he could understand that he's worth more than that. I gave him a sort of lecture, trying my best not to embarrass him. I explained to him that hurting another human being is a cowardly act, except when you're defending yourself. If you go around trying to fuck people up, you're just going to have a fucked up life. In the end, the only one who will really be fucked up is you. The kid got up and started to walk away. I went over to stop him from leaving and he paused. He complimented the jacket I was wearing and he sat back down. When the whole thing was over, I told him that I loved him and that there was more to life than violence and trying to act like a bigshot. I'm not sure how much he really heard, but he stayed for the rest of the seminar. I was happy I didn't shrug him off when he showed me what he wrote on that paper. He had written something demeaning and, I hope, I helped him to see that he deserved to have bigger dreams and plans.

Many kids are just confused, so adults have to deal with them with strength and kindness. You have to show kids that hard work can achieve their dreams, but that they can have fun doing it. A lot of kids have lost hope and they need heroes in their lives. These heroes don't have to be athletes or actors or celebrities - they really just need their parents. If their parents aren't around for whatever reason, then the community has to come together to support them and lead them in the right direction. I was deeply honored that I had this chance to be a role model to a new generation, and I look forward to getting the opportunity to inspire more kids in the future.

Chapter 16 - The Glow

"Nearly all men can stand adversity, but if you want to test a man's character, give him power. "

Abraham Lincoln

To me, life is all about energy. We all have good energy and bad energy. This is the reality and we should learn how best to deal with it. If you want to learn to create good energy, start by reflecting on your thoughts. I look even deeper than that, I look for what's in my heart, my honest feelings about something or someone.

You can't live your life all alone. Your life is filled with interactions with other people, and it's important to be aware that you are always connected with others. When you go to the store, you have to interact with a salesperson; when you want your car fixed, you have to interact with the mechanic; when you get married, you have to interact with your mate, and maybe your children, if you had any. There is no way around it. I learned to understand myself in a way that works better in this interactive world we live in. To help, I've read many books that have given me more enlightening ways of looking at life and that have truly made a difference for me. These books have put me on a deeper journey into self-discovery. I once took part in a curriculum at a program called Landmark Education. Landmark Education (now called Landmark Worldwide) offers personal development seminars and awareness training to help you realize your true potential, allowing for better relationships with both yourself and with others. I periodically continue to attend their seminars. I especially enjoyed and learned from Causing the Miraculous and Living Passionately seminars that were led by Gerri Newman.

We can learn about ourselves from our outlook on life. If we're honest about our judgments, resentments, and righteousness about a particular issue, it provides an understanding of who we are in society. Allowing ourselves to hear what others think of us, or, how we are projecting ourselves to other people, is helpful. They will acknowledge both our good points and bad points. If we can be gracious enough to not take any of what they say too personally, we can gain some valuable information that can help us on our journey. It's only an opinion after all, right? It would be helpful to avoid being defensive, and truly listen to these opinions because they have validity and may give you some great points of advice. If you can do that, you'll be a winner in life.

That leads me to the next topic: emotions. We can't function properly in life until we learn how to manage our emotions in a way that keeps us balanced. Our emotions are either derived from our spiritual self or, as like in most cases, from patterns that have been instilled in our minds from when we're very young. Our minds are like computers; they store images and memories from the past, and the mind attaches stories to those images. These stories make up our behavior. Let me give you some common examples to explain what I mean. You tell your boyfriend to make sure to put the seat down after he uses the toilet. He constantly forgets. Now, every time you see a toilet seat up, it reminds you of your boyfriend not putting it down. Or, you're about to park your car and someone pulls into the very space that you were about to pull into. What does this mean to you? What response does this trigger within you? How do you behave? A lot of these emotions are triggered by issues from our youth that we've never properly resolved.

You might notice that people have different responses to things. Your responses will tell you something about yourself, how you deal with different circumstances, and how you create the situations that you experience. I know, it's a crazy idea to say that we're creating our circumstances. But, I bet when you do something you're proud of you have no problem boasting, "Yeah, I did that!" It's the same when it comes to acknowledging everything else that you're responsible for.

Look at yourself as a rocket with an endless amount of fuel in it. When you have doubts in yourself, it's because you are basing your opinion from past experiences. In other words: who told you that you can't do something? Where was this thought created? How was it created? Where did you get these thoughts about yourself? These past thoughts don't *need* to be cemented into your mind. You will always have an opportunity to unravel them and create new experiences. However, that will only happen if you acknowledge that you are a huge part of creating those experiences. Once you acknowledge something, you can overcome it. Those stories about yourself are all attached to past experiences. They can be shattered... you are a rocket and you can soar like one. But to get to this place you have to put aside your ego and allow yourself to be vulnerable - only then can you learn.

A cup that is full has no more room to add to it. But a cup that is empty has all the room in the world to learn new things. We spend our life blaming other people for our circumstances. We behave as if we had no hand in how things fell into place in our life. We just go through life experiencing both the good and the bad, and just accept that this is all we can get out of life, this is all we can be. But we have the power to choose which things we want to put an effort into changing. Until we wise up, we play the game as if there's a limit to the amount of personal responsibility we can take. I think it would be a fun idea to take full responsibility for everything in our lives, even down to the bird flying over and crapping on our head. I believe there's a lesson to be learned in every area of life.

I also think it's important to go easy with it, though. Remember not to blame yourself too much. It's just like a game and it can be extremely fulfilling to just ride with life. It's exhausting to always go for the outcome and constantly live with questions like "What might happen if I do this?" I must admit, I have to think about these things too, but when our actions in life are always attached to an outcome, it can be a prison. I want to enjoy the game and if the outcome is a grand one, it will only be icing on the cake, but not the cake itself.

I'm now 51 years-old and just getting up every day to train is exciting for me, because I put things in my life that excite me. I feel like a little kid in a playground with so many wonderful things around. I respect my body and make sure to take care of it and not damage it.

Your body is something that you have to be grateful for. Sometimes, I look at Earth and all its inhabitants as one body, with energy flowing through it like blood. The planet's intention is to live freely with love, and that love is there for us whenever we're in a crisis. It's just like when the heart has an issue: all the different parts of your body get together to help it to survive, yet we have to take care of it so it works for us and not against us. We all have our ideas of what love is and we get caught up in the individual semantics, rather than thinking about simple acts of kindness.

There have been times when the people I love have done horrible things to me. I want to emphasize that I'm the one who saw these actions as horrible things...there's a hidden sense of blame in a phrase like "horrible things." There's a lot of baggage attached to it, and that baggage is usually very personal. However, every piece of baggage has many different interpretations. Other people will agree with some of your interpretations, yet others will not. I believe that the secret is to dismantle the adjectives that we place on our experiences, i.e. horrible, disgusting, hateful, cold, stupid, ignorant, and so on. If we can get away from those words, we can step back from blaming others.

If we looked at all the inhabitants on this earth as family members, then we would have a better chance of surviving and having an extraordinary life while living together on this big ball. Think about it… just one humongous family. Wow...that would be incredible, wouldn't it? Just the idea of it brings up all kinds of thoughts, concerns, and chances for excitement. How would a global family like that ever work? I agree. *How* would it work, exactly? I know how difficult it would be. When we think of our own family, there are family members we just don't meet eye to eye with. Some family members despise each other like enemies. I haven't spoken to some of my family members because of quarrels that we have had. But that's just part of what comes with being in a family - I would still never wish harm on any of the family members I've had issues with.

We have to recognize the fact that all families are dysfunctional in some way. Once we embrace that as a reality, we have the freedom to express ourselves in the situations that come about. When you resist something, it will persist and eventually expose itself. So if you think your family is "normal," then you have to eventually admit that maybe one of them is an alcoholic, or seriously needs anger management, or God forbid one might even be a gang member. Most likely there is a family member who has serious issues that they're dealing with.

A lot of time has gone by since *The Last Dragon* - 31 years to be exact. With more clarity in my life, I feel a new and fresh sense of urgency about how to generate and expand my career. Despite looking and feeling young, I haven't put much time into my social life since I found such new vigor in my career. Everything has been all work, all business. It's almost like I'm making up for lost time. Every time I come up to breathe, there's something else to do.

Most of my friends are married and have children. But it's different for an artist without a secure job. Life is a different journey for a creative person than for someone who went to school, got a degree, and has their financial life set in stone. Once careers are set, it seems like everyone puts their attention into creating a family. This is different than the life of most artists. It's the risk that a lot of artists take - it is a journey and one must know how to play it. It doesn't mean an artist can't have healthy and successful relationships. An artist just has to be more focused than the average person. They have to delicately manage their financial situation. An entertainer has to be clear about the Hollywood temptations and put things in perspective. Life is short and you can ruin your life if you don't put things in the right perspective.

One of the things I hope you can do after reading this book is to look at my experiences and learn from them. I want you to go beyond being the average human being. I also want to give this message to all artists: it's important to learn about the business of being an artist. If you focus on business and learn about financial management, it will allow you to focus on your craft.

Life has different categories of success. Spiritual success is having genuine peace within and being able to contribute to society with vigor and passion. Physical success is being physically healthy and having the ability to enjoy physical activities. Financial success can be great, with the right attitude of gratitude and giving back, but it can also create a superficial mask if you don't keep yourself grounded. You can gain certain notoriety and boost your ego, but it doesn't necessarily give you true success or allow you to achieve the sense of inner peace that so many people are seeking. That is more of a spiritual journey of looking within. There are a lot of spiritual treasures hidden throughout life...and at the same time, those treasures are right on the tip of your nose. One way is to learn to just let go. Having the ability to let go of attachments can generally help free your mind to truly listen and help you to feel your spirit within.

You need support to get to that level of peace. You need support so that you can be the best you can be, so that you can accomplish big and lofty dreams in life. It's just like how an Olympic athlete still needs a coach. You need a coach in life if you want to take it to another level. Let's face it, everything in your life thus far - your relationships, your career, your finances, your health - have all been made possible because of the knowledge that you've attained over time. If you want to take things to another level, you will have to gain a new kind of knowledge that you don't already have. In a word, you're going to have to be open to learning from others that are better at the thing you want to be better at.

So choose someone who knows you well, someone who knows the great things about you and the not-so-great things. Someone who knows you better than you know yourself. It must be someone you trust, possibly a trained professional therapist or a life coach, or choose someone that can inspire you to push yourself out of your comfort zone. If you don't completely trust them, how can you be brutally honest about yourself so that they can assist you in reaching your goals? They will push you to your limits. But don't resist their wisdom, submit to their advice and listen to them. They may put you on an emotional roller coaster ride, but then you can learn to enjoy the ride. When you hit walls (because you will), be open and don't give in to the blame game. When you focus your energy on blaming others, you are only giving your power away to someone else.

It's easy to find reasons for why things aren't working out for you. These *reasons* are only blocks that get in the way of you achieving what you want in your life, so don't give in to them. Don't let them become the *reasons* why you failed at the game of life. Take 100% responsibility for yourself. This way, you can own your entire life and take hold of it. In order to rise up to new heights, you need new knowledge. So go out there and attain it, the world is big!

You also need to acknowledge yourself and find supportive people who will acknowledge you. Sometimes the love and support of others can make you who you are. Muhammad Ali always had his team together to support him, and his assistant trainer, Drew Bundini Brown, would chant a mantra to him. It fired him up to believe he could achieve anything: "Float like a butterfly, sting like a bee, rumble, young man, rumble."

In some ways, how well we live life is decided by how well we deal with the imperfections of life. So have compassion for yourself and others. I use music for many different purposes, but I primarily use it to get me to shift my mood to an empowering one that has me at my best. Choose songs that diminish your bad attitude. Choose music that excites you, inspires you, and makes you laugh or cry. Play music that makes you feel courageous, unstoppable, relaxed and silent: music that makes you jump up and down and music that makes you as calm as a serene lake.

Unhealthy thoughts can take hold of your whole body. So let them go now! Build yourself up. The more you do the things you know you should do in life, the more you'll build the muscle of empowerment.

If you know that something is not for you, don't do it or you'll grow out of touch with your true self. Do what you know is good for you and your life. Focus on the wins in your life, even if you think they're small. Put your attention in this area and it *will* motivate you!

I'm deeply motivated when I look to the future and see everything that still lies ahead for me. I'm looking forward to working on other projects with my publisher Michael Conant, and I'd like to collaborate with Sony on doing a follow-up to *The Last Dragon*. I know that Sony has been impressed by the fact that we have sold out so many screenings of the film during my cross-country tour, and I would love do something exciting for the fans in the future. I also want to travel more overseas, I want to continue taking on interesting roles as an actor. I'm also looking forward to meeting someone who can be my partner in life. I've spent a lot of time over the past couple of years on this book and my other projects, and it's been a fulfilling but exhausting experience. Now that the book is complete, I'm excited to meet women that are up to inspiring things in their life. I'm patient, though. I know that special things are worth waiting for.

More than anything, I'm looking forward to fun and throwing myself into life. This isn't the end of my story...this is just the beginning. I think that your story is never really over. You can keep on writing it until the day you die. Even then, even when it seems your story is finally done, it's not, it still goes on.

The Last Dragon: Guardians of the Glow

Treatment

By Taimak and Danny MacDonald

The date is July 4th, 2018. We open our story at the Sumeru Temple in a secluded forest located in Japan. There's a religious ceremony taking place where 100 monks sing a hymn to praise Bishamonten, the Japanese God of Warriors. Standing tall on a pedestal is a glorious statue of Bishamonten, holding a jeweled naginata (wooden spear) in one hand and a small pagoda (bag) in the other hand. The statue is protected by a secured glass case. SIX ELDERS surround the shrine as they look down upon the other members. Sitting in front of the elders are YI CHENG (who represents Mind), YOSHI KAZUKI (who represents Body), and BRUCE LEROY (who represents Soul). Bruce Leroy is concerned when he notices that one of the elders has not attended the ceremony.

Meanwhile, in downtown New York City, two young men cut past the long line of people trying to get into a popular nightclub called Chilla. The two young men are CHRISTIAN, 17, good-looking and hip, and ANTONIO, 18, Latino and trendy. Christian has no idea why they're even trying to get into this club. They're underage and don't have fake IDs. Antonio tells Christian not to worry as he slips the DOOR GUY a one-hundred dollar bill and they are let in. Christian doesn't know how Antonio makes his extra cash, but he wants in. Antonio tells him his business is expanding into different territories and could use Christian's help. Antonio says, "It beats working at a pizza place, Papa Negro."

Back at the Temple, Bruce Leroy feels like something isn't right. He looks over at Yi Cheng, who is meditating. Yi Cheng gives off a strong green glow while he chants the hymn. Bruce Leroy knows something's wrong when he notices Yi Cheng's strong green glow transform an eerie black cloud.

In one of the temple corridors, we see ELDERLY WOMEN tied up with MASKED HENCHMEN holding swords to their throats. The MISSING ELDER is being held against his will as he's interrogated by a LEAD HENCHMAN. The Lead Henchman keeps asking the elder, "Who's the guardian of the seventh jewel?" The elder cries and only replies, "You told me not to tell, Master! The vow of silence is taken to the grave!" The Lead Henchman slices one of the elder's ears off with a quick swipe of his sword. The ear falls to the ground as the elder's mouth is covered by the Henchmen to mute his screams.

Inside of Chilla, Christian notices DJ SHAYLA, 23, sexy, spinning the turn tables and emceeing to the crowd that has gathered to celebrate the Fourth of July. Christian is mesmerized by Shayla's beauty. Antonio nudges Christian and says, "That's DJ Shayla, the spinstress of Soho. My cousin is friends with her. I'll introduce you. After all, you have a lot in common, she spins records and you spin pizzas." Antonio laughs and he leads Christian towards Shayla.

While Antonio moves through the crowd, he tries to discreetly deal ecstasy to club hoppers. We realize that he's a drug dealer.

From his office, IDRIS oversees the club and observes Antonio slinging drugs. Idris, who is in his 30's, is the big, muscular, flashy, black mafia boss and club owner of Chilla. Idris whispers to one of his GOONS.

Back in Japan, Bruce Leroy quietly excuses himself from the ceremony and carefully investigates the corridors as he searches for the missing elder.

In New York, a crowd surrounds Christian, making it difficult to get closer to DJ Shayla. Christian hollers to get DJ Shayla's attention. Shayla's on the microphone and spots Christian. She asks him, "You got a request?" Christian says, "Yeah, your number." She smiles and says, "That's not the first time I've heard that line." Christian replies, "As beautiful as you are, I bet you hear it every day." Shayla responds playfully, "Don't you want to show me you're different? Why recycle a bad pick-up line?" Christian charmingly says, "Because you haven't had the right guy say it to you yet." Shayla sarcastically retorts, "Well, let me know when Prince Charming gets here." The crowd laughs at Christian. The chemistry between the two is electrifying as they stare into each other's eyes.

While they flirt, Idris' goons grab Antonio and Christian and drag them out of the club. DJ Shayla looks on concerned, but continues to please the crowd.

At the Sumeru Temple, the Lead Henchman yells at the elder: "I need to know where it is! That's why I've risen from the grave. The temple's in great danger. Where's the seventh jewel?" The Lead Henchmen throws the elder to the ground. The elder cries out, "I'm old and weak. Why are you doing this, Master?" The Lead Henchman stomps on one of the Elder's hands and we hear bones crack. He warns the elder for a final time: "Stop disobeying your Master! This is the last time I'm asking! Who's the guardian?" The elder sobs as he says, "Zhi Yong."

The Lead Henchmen takes off his mask and smiles: the Lead Henchman is actually Yi Cheng. He laughs and says, "Elders are supposed to be wise beyond their years. I guess your years are up. You did good, old man." The elder stares in shock as he replies, "Yi Cheng? You'll never get your hands on the power in time!" Yi Cheng responds, "Too bad you won't be around to find out." One of the other masked henchmen, MING TAO, stabs the elder with his dagger.

Bruce Leroy notices the commotion and locks eyes with the smiling Yi Cheng. Bruce Leroy sprints towards the henchmen and starts fighting them. In an instant, Yi Cheng vanishes in mid air and we cut back to the religious ceremony where Yi Cheng's dark glow fades. He looks around and yells, "Now!" DOZENS of MASKED HENCHMEN crash the religious ceremony and attack the temple. Yoshi, who possesses a defensive blue glow, defends the elders from weapons that are fired towards them.

Back in the alley behind Chilla, Idris's top soldier, MALIK, tells Antonio that he has disrespected Idris by dealing drugs in his territory. Antonio says he wants to be partners and that he will give a cut of his money to Idris. Malik tells Antonio that Idris doesn't negotiate with anyone and he needs to be made an example of. The goons jump Antonio and Christian and start to beat them up.

The fight scenes taking place at the Temple and Chilla are intercut with one another as we watch Bruce Leroy and Christian fighting at the same time. Bruce Leroy possesses the power of the golden glow while he fights off henchmen, who all possess low voltage glows that are dimly colored. Christian, who fights like he's had some Kung Fu training, defends himself for a few moments until Malik, a skilled fighter, steps up to fight him. Bruce Leroy uses a variety of skillful moves to defeat his opponents, but it's just the opposite case for Christian. We see Christian getting beat down by Malik.

After being pummeled by the goons, Antonio shouts from the ground, "Leave him alone! He doesn't have anything to do with this. Just let him go!" Malik walks over to Antonio and glances back at Christian. Defenseless, Christian watches Malik give Antonio a powerful kick to the nose that instantly kills him. Malik says to Christian, "Tell everyone you know…Idris doesn't want anyone but his men slinging in his city. And if you want to live, stay away from his girl, Shayla. She's Idris' property."

In the midst of chaos at the Sumeru Temple, Yi Cheng breaks the sacred glass of Bishamonten's statue and steals the heavenly jeweled spear. Bruce Leroy and Yoshi continue to fight off all of the enemies as Yi's henchmen set the temple on fire and escape. Leroy drags the elder out of the burning temple, and with his last breath he looks up at Leroy and says, "I'm sorry…Zhi Yong. I'm sor..." This moment is intercut with the alley back in New York, where Christian cries as he holds Antonio in his arms.

FADE OUT.

TITLE UP: THE LAST DRAGON: GUARDIANS OF THE GLOW

FADE IN:

We see what remains of the Sumeru Temple as the surviving members try to clean up the mess. Bruce Leroy and Yoshi stand before the six remaining elders. The WISE ELDER explains that Yi Cheng used his power of the mind to create an illusion and appear to be the Elders' old master. The Heavenly Jeweled Spear that he stole, also known as the Ame-No-Nuboko, was given to mankind by the Gods. Its power is limitless. If the man who holds it already possesses a glow within him, he will become a God, strong enough to defeat armies single-handedly and take over the world.

The Gods originally gave the spear to mankind as a way to create new land. One touch of the spear's tip could even raise an entire country from the sea. The Gods then let mankind keep it as an emergency precaution. If there was ever a situation where evil threatened to take over the world, the Heavenly Jeweled Spear could be used by a noble warrior to protect the land. It is, without a doubt, the most valuable weapon in the Universe.

In the beginning, the Gods gave the responsibility of protecting the Ame-No-Nuboko to Bishamonten. Bishamonten realized that the spear's power was generated by seven jewels that represent the seven planets of the Ancients. He decided to divide the seven jewels all over the world and delegated them to warriors who were worthy enough to protect them. Since the beginning of time, these guardians have been protecting the sacred jewels and passing on the responsibility to other warriors who have been able to handle the responsibility. Over the past seven years, Guardians have been murdered all over the world and six of the sacred jewels were stolen. We see flashbacks that show Yi Cheng slaughtering the guardians.

Hearing all of this, Yoshi is confused and asks, "Why now?" It turns out that the Gods originally agreed to give mankind the Heavenly Jeweled Spear for only 21 centuries. This math is based on the Universal combination of the 7 ancient planets, 7 jewels, and the 7 Japanese Gods of Fortune. The Gods decided that if man could survive 21 centuries on their own, they would no longer need the Ame-No-Nuboko.

Now, on 7/7/14 at 7:14 in the morning, there will be a 7 minute total solar eclipse during which the sun's power will be blocked by the moon. This will leave all who possess the glow absolutely powerless. If the Ame-No-Nuboko's power isn't activated before the total eclipse ends, the weapon will be taken back by the Gods and mankind will be helpless. It's the classic case of "The Gods giveth and the Gods taketh away."

Many people believed that this story was a myth. Yi Cheng, however, knew that it was true. Yi Cheng chose to train at the Sumeru Temple, because that was where the Heavenly Jeweled Spear was enshrined. This gave him time to strategically create his master plan: it was only a matter of time before his evil would show its face and he would attempt to steal the magical blade.

Bruce Leroy and Yoshi simply can't believe Yi Cheng betrayed them and the Universe. The three of them were supposed to represent the powers of Mind, Body, and Soul, protecting the Universe from evil, not trying to use its power for evil purposes. Bruce Leroy asks, "Why did the elder say the name, Zhi Yong?" The Wise Elder responds, "Zhi Yong is the guardian of the seventh jewel." Bruce Leroy informs the elders that Zhi Yong was his master and he never mentioned the jewel to him. The Wise Elder tells Leroy that, before he passed, Zhi Yong mentioned a disciple child with great intelligence. Leroy is dumbfounded and then he suddenly thinks of his nephew: "Was he talking about Christian?"

Zhi Yong died seven years ago, and now Yi Cheng will try to track down anyone associated with Master Zhi Yong to find the jewel. It seems likely that Christian has some connection to the jewel, and Yi Cheng will do his best to hunt him down. Bruce Leroy and Yoshi have less than a week to go back to Harlem, protect Bruce's family, and stop Yi Cheng from getting his hands on the final jewel. They'll split up: Yoshi will search for Yi Cheng and Bruce Leroy will search for the jewel.

Yi Cheng stands in a vaulted room with the Heavenly Jeweled Spear at his side. He places the sixth jewel on the sacred naginata and stares at the open slot reserved for the seventh jewel. He shouts that time is ticking away and he tells his henchmen to search throughout all of Harlem. He wants them to rip the city limb by limb to find the precious jewel before the solar eclipse.

In a small apartment in Harlem, SOPHIA, 35, Christian's mom, makes breakfast while Christian sits depressed at the kitchen table. Sophia owns the family pizza place, Big Daddy Green's Pizza, where Christian works after school. Christian is dressed in a cheap suit and tie, because he has to go to Antonio's wake. His mom is worried about him and she examines his bruises. Sophia thinks he should focus on his senior year of high school so he can get a scholarship to college. She is disappointed that he quit the school's track team. He was actually a state champion and that could have been his ticket to a scholarship.

Christian gives Sophia a wiseass response and Sophia tells him he has to work at the pizza place tomorrow because she needs to go to the bank for a loan. She needs the loan so that she can make her payments on the pizza joint. This pisses Christian off, but Sophia responds with a momly, "If you're not going to college, you're gonna have to help with the family business." Christian responds with attitude: "What family?" At that moment, Bruce Leroy knocks on the door and Sophia is thrilled to see her brother. Christian is not so happy about Bruce's appearance. He tells Leroy to go screw himself and walks out the door.

Yi Cheng's Henchmen break into Zhi Yong's old apartment and dojo. His brother, OGAMI YONG, an older man, is jumped by the Henchmen and interrogated just like the elder from the temple. He's clueless and harmless but that doesn't stop the Henchmen from beating him senseless. They tear the place apart, looking for any clues that might lead to the jewel, until they come across a photo of Zhi Yong, Bruce Leroy, and a 10 YEAR-OLD CHRISTIAN.

Sophia tells Leroy how worried she is that Christian is getting involved with the wrong crowd and that he almost got himself killed while hanging out with Antonio. Sophia has had a rough time in the past few years. She got pregnant at 18 and her boyfriend, Christian's dad, was killed in Iraq before Christian was born. Big Daddy Green passed a few years later, Mama Green relocated to Florida, Richie's doing his own thing in Los Angeles, and Leroy left the country to go on a secret mission. Sophie has been alone this entire time and things have been hard for her. Leroy feels bad that Sophia had to raise Christian on her own and tells her why he had to leave.

We see a flashback of Master Zhi Yong on his deathbed. Zhi Yong tells Bruce Leroy that he's only just beginning to learn about the power of the glow. There are different levels to mastering the glow, and each level can allow a fighter to gain different superpowers. These powers come from the visible planets in the Universe. For instance, the Mind is ruled by Mercury and grants the powers of illusion and deception. The Body is ruled by Earth and grants the power of a defensive glow that is unable to be penetrated by any weapon. The Soul is ruled by the sun and grants the powers of energy and velocity. There's a place in Japan called the Sumeru Temple where warriors of all martial art backgrounds train and build on mastering the different powers of the glow. This is where the most powerful weapon in the world is enshrined and protected by great warriors.

Master Zhi Yong's dying request is for Bruce Leroy to continue his training at the Sumeru Temple. He also requests that Bruce keep his destination a secret from his friends and family. It's too dangerous for anyone to know his location and he must leave everyone and everything behind. He tells Bruce that "It's the responsibility of every great master to make sacrifices for the greater good of the world." Bruce Leroy would never dishonor his master. He agrees to the dying man's wishes and he embarks on a journey to Japan.

Back in the present, Christian goes to Antonio's wake and sits alone in the back of the funeral home. DJ Shayla shows up and takes a seat next to Christian. They walk home together. Shayla tells Christian how sorry she is about Antonio. Christian tells her that he won't let Idris get away with what happened. He's going to take down Idris' whole operation and do it all by himself if he has to. Shayla tries to talk him out of it because she doesn't want him to get killed. Idris is untouchable and has powerful connections that could squash Christian like a bug.

Yoshi investigates Chinatown and asks around about Yi Cheng. Nobody wants to talk about Yi Cheng. Everyone is afraid that Yi Cheng will learn that they gave Yoshi information and he will murder their families. A group of SMALL-TIME HOODS are performing a Tae Kwon Do musical routine in front of a small crowd on a popular street corner. Yoshi tries to walk around them, but trips and accidentally ruins the dance. This angers the hoods and they try to beat him down. Yoshi tries to avoid a confrontation, but they picked the wrong guy to mess with and he teaches them a physical lesson. He asks the hoods about Yi Cheng, but they are too scared to respond for a few moments. One of the hoods finally tells him to go to Tao Enterprises building, because the people there will definitely know where to find Yi Cheng.

That night, Christian tries to sneak back into his apartment through the roof when he stumbles on Leroy meditating. Leroy tells him that he's sorry for the loss of his friend and tries to give him words of wisdom about going down the right path in life. Christian doesn't care to hear anything that Bruce Leroy has to say and he blows him off.

Yi Cheng is training when he's interrupted by his Henchmen. Ming Tao hands him the photo of Bruce Leroy, Zhi Yong, and Young Christian. The picture is the only clue from Zhi Yong's old dojo that might lead Yi Cheng to the rare seventh jewel. Cheng's not surprised to see that Bruce Leroy is connected to the Heavenly Jeweled Spear. He always knew that Universe would bring the warriors of Mind, Body, and Soul together for an epic battle that would decide the fate of the world.

The next day, Christian works at Big Daddy Green's Pizza place. The joint is busy as tons of people line up for a slice. Christian puts on a show as he does different Karate moves while he spins the dough. Some LOCAL ITALIANS make fun of the idea of a black kid using martial arts moves to make pizza. Meanwhile, we see the news on TV: a huge mob of protestors stand by the water in Bayside, Brooklyn, and a REPORTER stands in front of the mob. The reporter interviews Ming Tao, the face of Tao Enterprises. Ming Tao talks about the fact that Tao Enterprises is reconstructing Brooklyn by the waterfront, buying up properties and building new developments. This is happening in the area where Big Daddy Green's Pizza is located. Christian makes a snide comment: "Man, Tao Enterprises is trying to take over the world with all the land they're buying."

Bruce Leroy walks in and notices how busy it is. He offers to help and makes a fool of himself along the way. Bruce Leroy is a martial arts master, but he can't run a pizza place to save his life. The fact that Bruce Leroy is a total goofball and has such poor pizza skills makes Christian smile. He temporarily loses his negative attitude. But as soon as Christian feels like he's opening up to Bruce Leroy, he puts up his guard again. He snarls at him: "You think you can come back into my life after 7 years and act like nothing happened? People needed you here and you left. I didn't realize that a guy who can catch bullets with his teeth could be such a coward!" Sophia walks in as Christian storms out. Sophia didn't get the loan that she wanted from the bank. The bank is now owned by Tao Enterprises and they want all of the old tenants out.

Inside Chilla, DJ Shayla sits by herself, calmly spinning music. Malik suddenly cuts off the power. He tells her that Idris wants to speak with her. Shayla walks into Idris' office as TWO SEXY LADIES walk out. Shayla watches as Idris puts his clothes back on. Idris tells her if she wants to become a big star, she needs to completely devote herself to him. He knows about the "boy" that she walked home from the funeral with. Shayla's is defensive because she doesn't like to be followed and Idris doesn't own her. She works for him and that's as far as the relationship will ever go. Idris puts a gorgeous necklace around Shayla's neck and tells her that many men had to die for jewelry like this...and it would be a shame if more had to die. He tells Shayla that if he sees her with another guy again, he'll kill him and mangle her pretty little face so that no other man will ever want her. Shayla leaves the room as fast as she can. As she leaves, Malik enters and says a Japanese gangster has the jewel that Yi Cheng has been looking for.

Christian hangs out in Bruce Leroy's abandoned dojo. The building looks like it's been demolished. Christian looks at a picture of Bruce Leroy, Zhi Yong, and a 10 year-old Christian, the exact same picture that Ming Tao found at Master Zhi Yong's apartment. Bruce Leroy walks in and is not surprised to see Christian there. He figured that he might find him here. Bruce Leroy starts talking about the past and how much he enjoyed mentoring Christian. He didn't want to leave the country and leave them all behind, but he had to. It was for everyone's safety that his location remained unknown. He notices the photo Christian is holding and talks about the time they spent at Master Zhi Yong's Maze of Destiny.

We see a flashback to seven years earlier. We are in upstate New York, where Master Zhi Yong and Leroy hold a training exercise for Christian at a mysterious hedge maze called the Maze of Destiny. The ten year-old Christian fights through many obstacles as he runs through the maze. He runs into different statues of lions, tigers, and dragons at every dead end. He moves quickly and shows great intelligence as he finds his way out of the maze faster than anyone that Zhi Yong had ever seen.

Zhi Yong tells Christian: "Every decision one makes, will lead you down a certain path. Sometimes you must go back to move forward, right or wrong is not the answer. It's about following the path that will lead you to your destiny. You have incredible instincts and speed. It's your ability to use those instincts without thinking that will give you strength. Always keep your mind clear and play freely as you do now and you'll be able to run the maze blindfolded." Master Zhi Yong hands Christian a prize for finishing the maze. It's a Japanese puzzle box that's been in his family for many years. The puzzle requires many different moves to open: only those who possess a "natural mind" can solve the complicated puzzle.

Back at the dojo, Bruce Leroy tells Christian he was one of the fastest runners he ever saw. Christian shrugs. Leroy notices something on the floor of the dojo: it's the Japanese puzzle box that Zhi Yong gave to Christian. Christian left it in the dojo a few years earlier. He was bitter about Zhi Yong's death and Leroy's absence, and he wanted to throw away everything that might remind him of the old days. Leroy picks up the dusty puzzle box and starts playing with it. Christian takes it from him, annoyed. Christian never even figured out how to open it and he generally just blames Bruce Leroy for the way that his life turned out.

Christian is upset as he says: "My dad died before I was born, Grandpa died soon after and the only person I could rely on in my life was you, my Uncle Leroy. You and Master Zhi Yong spent time training me and I was happy. All I wanted to do was become a great master like you. Then Master Zhi Yong dies and you disappear like it was nothing. I was ten years-old. I realized nobody gives a shit about me at the end of the day and I don't give a shit about anybody else."

Bruce Leroy tells him he has always cared about him, his mom cares about him, and Master Zhi Yong cared about him as well. He understands how difficult life has been for Christian since he left, but he's here now and he needs Christian's help. Time is of the essence, so Bruce Leroy asks if Zhi Yong ever told Christian anything about a sacred jewel. However, Christian has no idea what he's talking about. He tells Bruce: "If I did know where it was, I wouldn't tell you anyways."

Tao Enterprises is located in a high rise building in Manhattan. Yoshi goes undercover as a janitor and sneaks around the building. In the elevator, he meets the eyes of a group of well-dressed businessmen and we see quick flashbacks of the battle at the Sumeru Temple. Yoshi realizes the businessmen were the Henchmen from the battle. The elevator stops at the 20th floor. The businessmen get off the elevator and Yoshi follows them. Ming Tao opens the door to a large boardroom and the businessmen walk in. Yoshi is about to follow them when he's cut off by a MAINTENANCE SUPERVISOR, who tells Yoshi there's a mess in the bathroom that he has to clean up. Yoshi quickly gets a glimpse of what's happening in the boardroom. There is a large monitor at the head of the conference table, and Yoshi sees Yi Cheng's face on the screen. He overhears Yi Cheng ask his men for all of the information that they have gathered on Zhi Yong and Bruce Leroy.

Yoshi follows the Maintenance Supervisor into the bathroom. He tries to quietly escape from the Maintenance Supervisor, who wants to teach him how to properly unclog a toilet. He sneaks into one of the bathroom vents and starts crawling towards the boardroom.

Meanwhile, Idris and his men interrupt Yi Cheng's meeting. Idris bows to Yi Cheng and refers to him as Master. We find out Idris was trained by the mighty Yi Cheng. Idris claims that he has found the seventh jewel. He tells Yi Cheng that a Japanese gangster named Sato Kazajuri bought it from the gravedigger who buried Zhi Yong. Apparently, Zhi Yong had the jewel located in a secret compartment inside the coffin but the clumsy gravedigger fell onto the coffin and the compartment smashed open, revealing the sacred jewel. Yoshi listens to the conversation through the vents. Yi Cheng praises Idris and tells him that money is no object and that he should pay Sato whatever he wants for the jewel. Once he has all the power in the world, Idris can have any continent he wants for his very own.

Christian waits outside of Shayla's apartment until he sees her walking down the street. He stops her and tells her to stay away from Chilla's back alley tonight. Shayla is concerned and she tells him to reconsider anything he's about to do. At that moment, Malik pulls up with his goons. They see Christian and decide that's finally time to kill him off. Malik warned him to stay away from Shayla, so now Christian has got to die. Bruce Leroy shows up and helps to fight the goons. Christian holds his own against these enemies, until Malik connects on a roundhouse kick to the head. Bruce Leroy takes on Malik and Malik is no match for the far more advanced Bruce Leroy. Shayla is impressed by Leroy's skill. Christian notices that Shayla is impressed by Leroy, and he takes off in a jealous fit. Leroy looks around and realizes Christian is gone. He asks Shayla if she saw where he went. She doesn't know and Leroy tells Shayla to come with him.

It's nighttime and Chilla is bumping as club hoppers tear up the dance floor. Idris sits in his office. He calls Shayla and leaves her a voicemail message, asking her why she's not at the club. He says that if she doesn't show up soon, he's gonna track her down and she will wish that she was never born.

In the back alley, SATO KAZAJURI, all pimped out, gets out of his flashy car. He holds a briefcase. We see the rest of his MEN pile out of the car with heavy artillery. In a quick flash, Yoshi appears out of the darkness. He is dressed in a mail carriers' uniform. He says he has a letter for a Mr. Sato and Sato asks, "From whom?" Sato instantly distrusts Yoshi and orders his men to kill this fool. The goons unleash rounds of ammunition on Yoshi, but Yoshi uses his glow to shield himself from the bullets. Yoshi takes down Sato and his men. He opens the briefcase and eyes the jewel. He picks it up and looks it over, and then he realizes that it's a fake.

A bloodied Malik stumbles into Idris' office and relates what happened at Shayla's place. Idris is furious and wants Bruce Leroy's head. One of Idris' other goons apologizes for interrupting, but he says that there's a guy named Sato Kazajuri here to see him. Idris is pissed at the situation but he'll handle Bruce Leroy later. As for now, they've got a deal to get done.

At Sophia's apartment, Bruce Leroy, Sophia, and Shayla sit in the kitchen. Bruce Leroy wants them to find a safe place to stay. Shayla can't believe she's gotten caught up in this situation. Sophia tells her to get used to it if she's going to hang out with any of the Green men. Leroy has to find Christian because he knows that he's in great danger. Shayla tells Leroy that Christian is going to go to Chilla, because he wants to kill Idris and Malik. Leroy tells the girls to go to his old dojo. The building is abandoned and there are weapons there if they need to protect themselves. Before the girls can finish discussing where they should go, Bruce Leroy is gone like the wind.

Meanwhile, Christian buys a gun from a RANDOM GANGBANGER in front of a sketchy area in Brooklyn.

Idris, his men, and Cheng's henchmen meet Sato Kazajuri in the back alley. However, it's not really Sato: it's Yoshi, dressed in Sato's clothes and posing as him. Idris says that he respects Sato for coming alone. Idris thinks that this shows Sato is either very trusting or incredibly stupid. Idris asks Sato about the gravedigger who he bought the jewel from and Yoshi makes up a ridiculous story. While the deal goes down, we see Christian slowly creep up behind a dumpster with a loaded gun in his hand. He aims towards Idris and is about to shoot when suddenly Bruce Leroy quickly grabs him and pulls him back. Bruce Leroy whispers to Christian, "We need Idris alive so he can lead us to Yi Cheng."

Yoshi says he wants to personally deliver the jewel to Yi Cheng. Idris says, "Nobody meets the man. Come to think of it, nobody mentioned the man. How do you know Master Cheng?" Idris gets a good look at the jewel in Yoshi's hands and realizes it's a fake. Leroy tells Christian to stay there and he rushes out from his hiding place. A battle breaks out which pits Bruce Leroy and Yoshi against Idris and his Henchmen. Idris, who possesses a dark purplish glow, squares off against the brightly glowing Bruce Leroy, while Yoshi takes down Malik and the other Henchmen. Idris escapes, leaving the whereabouts of Yi Cheng's location still a mystery.

Idris tells Yi Cheng that the meeting was a trap and the jewel was a fake. Yoshi and Bruce Leroy got the better of them. Yi Cheng says, "Time is running out! If I want something done, I'll have to do it myself. They no longer have to worry about finding me...because I'm going to find them." Yi Cheng is going to send Henchmen from many different martial arts backgrounds to track down Bruce Leroy and his family. He opens his office door and there are hundreds of soldiers training. He shouts, "Release the dogs."

Bruce Leroy is upset with Christian for trying to kill Idris. Christian is upset with Bruce Leroy because he thinks he was trying to steal Shayla from him. He tells him that this is not the time for such childish jealousy and he reluctantly introduces Christian to Yoshi. They speculate that Master Zhi Yong must have buried himself with a fake jewel as a decoy to buy some time for the guardians to find the real one. Yoshi speculates that Christian must somehow know where the jewel is. Zhi Yong would never have mentioned a young protégé to the wise elders unless his comment had something to do with the jewel. Christian wonders whether he might also be a decoy. In any case, the group knows that have become targets for Yi Cheng and Idris. They need to get back to the abandoned dojo immediately.

While Sophia and Shayla are on their way to the abandoned dojo, Sophia decides to stop at the pizza place for supplies. As soon as they're about to walk into the pizza joint, the restaurant EXPLODES into flames! Cop cars quickly pull up to the scene. A first, the girls are relieved that the police have arrived. Unfortunately, they suddenly realize that these aren't actual cops. Idris and dozens of his ninja soldiers step out of the cop cars. They're here to kidnap Sophia and Shayla.

Bruce Leroy, Yoshi, and Christian show up to the dojo. Yi Cheng calls Christian's cell phone and tells him that he has kidnapped Sophia and Shayla. Cheng says: "You've got until sunrise to give me the jewel or I start torturing mommy…and your girlfriend will be passed around like fresh meat." While Yi Cheng speaks on the phone, Idris explains to Shayla that she'll have to obey his every command when this is all over.

Bruce Leroy, Yoshi, and Christian try to come up with a plan to stop Yi Cheng and save the ladies. Yoshi sits down next to Christian and tells him a story about Zhi Yong, who was his uncle and a man who he loved deeply. Yoshi trained with Zhi Yong for many years and he knew him very well. Zhi Yong was able to look into people's hearts and he had great wisdom. Yoshi thinks that Zhi Yong chose Christian to guard the sacred jewel, because he knew that there was someone who would always protect Christian at all costs: Bruce Leroy. In a way, Bruce would be the guardian of the jewel. Yoshi tells Christian that he needs to focus and that he must think back to anything Master Zhi Yong might've said about the jewel.

As Christian thinks, he plays with the old puzzle box. He thinks about what Zhi Yong said when he gave it to him. Christian focuses until he finally opens it and finds a 10,000 year-old fortune cookie. He breaks it open and reads the fortune. It reads: "The dragon's greatest strength is his jewel of knowledge." Just before the sun rises over the city, Christian figures out where the jewel is. It will be a suicide mission, but it's the only shot they have.

Bruce Leroy calls Yi Cheng. He says that they will make a trade: the girls for the jewel. They will meet at the Maze of Destiny, where there will be no way out. Yi Cheng agrees and hangs up the phone. Yi Cheng tells his men that they can make the trade, but that it doesn't really matter in the end. Once Yi Cheng has all the power, his enemies will be dead.

THE BIG FINALE

We see the sun rising as Bruce Leroy, Yoshi, and Christian run through the hedge maze. They search for a particular dragon statue that Christian saw in the maze when he was a kid. Yi Cheng shows up outside of the maze with his army and looks at his watch. It reads: 7:00 AM. His henchmen have Sophia and Shayla tied up. Yi Cheng tells his men to block off the entire maze so that our heroes can't get out alive, and he orders them to find the jewel as quickly as they can. There are only 14 more minutes until the solar eclipse.

Like ants cluttering into an ant farm, Henchmen of all different fighting styles and weapons attack the maze. Christian stops in the middle of the maze because he's lost. Henchmen start approaching Christian, Bruce Leroy and Yoshi. Bruce Leroy and Yoshi fight them off while Christian continues through the maze. Yoshi fights to get to the hostages. Idris wants a piece of Yoshi and he tells his henchmen to back off because he wants to take care of him by himself. Christian finally reaches the dragon statue and opens its head to reveal the final jewel.

Bruce Leroy destroys Ming Tao and fights his way towards Christian. The moon gets closer to the sun. Malik wants to be the one to give the jewel to Yi Cheng, so he tells Christian to hand it over before he gets his ass kicked again. Christian fights Malik and this time defeats him. He has the jewel and sprints towards the exit, when he suddenly runs into Bruce. Bruce tells him the women are safe and that Christian should give him the jewel. Christian is unsure what to do, when Bruce Leroy says, "You have nothing to fear. Trust your uncle like Master Zhi Yong trusted you." Christian hands over the jewel. Bruce Leroy transforms into Yi Cheng. He pulled a mind trick on Christian by posing as Bruce Leroy. Yi Cheng laughs hysterically as he looks to the sky and watches the moon block out the sun…its 7:14 AM.

Meanwhile, Yoshi defeats Idris and then loses his glow. Bruce Leroy's golden glow fades as well and he has no choice but to surrender to the ninja soldiers when they point their guns at him.

Through a cloud of darkness, the ninja army brings all of the prisoners forward so that they can witness Yi Cheng place the final jewel on the Ame-No-Nuboko. Bruce Leroy asks why a man with all the riches and power of Mercury would turn to a life of evil. Yi Cheng says, "Because I want it all! As long as there's money, land,

and power, there's always going to be someone who wants it. And that man is me. Or should I say…that GOD is me! I've built my army from the ground up and will take the great city of New York first. After that, the world will have no choice but to follow me or accept the fate of extinction! The Gods gave us this power and now they want to take it back? No, I don't think so. Be prepared to bow to your King!"

Yi Cheng places the jewel in the naginata, but nothing happens. Christian gave Yi Cheng a fake jewel. We see a flashback of Christian grabbing the fake jewel during the fight in the alley. Christian escapes from the goons that hold him down and sprints through the now pitch black maze. Yi Cheng charges after Christian and yells, "Get him! There's not much time!" Bruce Leroy and Yoshi fight against the remaining soldiers and they defeat them. Leroy and Yoshi don't need any superpowers to defeat these guys, because they're naturally great fighters. They free the girls and Bruce Leroy tells Yoshi to get them to a safe place while he tracks down Christian.

As Christian runs through the maze, he hears Master Zhi Yong's words in his head: "It's your ability to use those instincts without thinking that will give you strength. Always keep your mind clear and play freely as you do now and you'll be able to run the maze blindfolded." Christian smiles as he speeds around the maze and avoids the Henchmen.

Bruce Leroy runs up to Yi Cheng and challenges him. He wants to fight Yi Cheng one on one, without any superpowers. Yi Cheng tells his men to find Christian and he says that he'll deal with Bruce

Leroy. Yi Cheng and Bruce Leroy have an epic battle with naginatas. Bruce Leroy snatches the Heavenly Jeweled Spear from Yi Cheng and knocks him on his back, but hesitates to kill him. Yi Cheng is cocky as he shouts, "You're too pure to kill me, soul glow! And if you do, it doesn't matter anyways. Look around you." Bruce Leroy notices Cheng's soldiers have him surrounded at gunpoint. Cheng laughs: "Go ahead, kill me. You're dead anyways. Do you think you can defeat an army all by yourself?"

At that moment, Christian pops his head out of the bushes and says, "Uncle Leroy, here!" Christian tosses Bruce Leroy the seventh jewel and Bruce places it on the spear. Bruce Leroy transforms into the spitting image of Bishamonten. The magical naginata shoots a powerful golden ray and it destroys all of Yi Cheng's army. Yi Cheng shouts from the ground, "It wasn't supposed to be you! It was supposed to be me!" Bruce Leroy looks down at him and says, "It was supposed to be me. I'm the punisher of evildoers. I'm the Guardian of the Glow." Bruce Leroy, imbued with the power of Bishamonten, kills Yi Cheng. Bruce immediately puts down the heavenly weapon and transforms back into his normal self as the sun comes out from behind the moon.

Bruce Leroy hugs Christian and asks how he knew that Yi Cheng was impersonating him. Christian says, "You'd never ask me to trust you…you always know that I do." Bruce Leroy tells him how proud of him he is. Yoshi, Sophia, and Shayla all run up to Christian and Leroy, overjoyed. In the end, it took the powers of Mind (Christian), Body (Yoshi), and Soul (Bruce Leroy) to outsmart Yi Cheng and save the world.

THE COOL ENDING

We see shots of Bruce Leroy and Yoshi giving the naginata back to the elders at the Sumeru Temple. Sophia gets an insurance check from the bank. Christian hangs up the photo of himself, Uncle Leroy, and Master Zhi Yong in his bedroom. DJ Shayla spins by herself in Chilla. Finally, Tao Enterprises has gone bankrupt.

There's a sign in front of the Chilla nightclub that reads: "Under New Management! Welcome to our Grand Opening!" Everyone's inside the club, celebrating. Christian walks in, dressed sharply and carrying a bouquet of flowers in his hands. He sees DJ Shayla hugging Bruce Leroy and he thinks that she wants him. Christian turns back around to leave, when DJ Shayla suddenly announces over the microphone: "Hey, Christian, could you teach me some moves?" Christian's shocked and he asks, "Me?" DJ Shayla and Christian share an intimate kiss. Yoshi dances with a couple of beautiful ladies and they all drag Bruce Leroy to the dance floor to join them.

FINAL SCENE THAT LEADS INTO THE SEQUEL

We see a big, tall, intimidating figure walking out of jail. He has his back turned to us as the prison gates open. We see a handful of black town cars pull up in front of him. Malik and Idris' remaining goons stand in front of the cars. Malik walks up to this imposing ex-con and tells him that their henchmen were massacred. Malik barely got away alive. He breaks the bad news about the ex-con's brother, Idris – he's been killed.

The ex-con beats Malik to a pulp and yells, "Who did it?" Malik responds, "It was Bruce Leroy." The angry man knocks Malik out with a powerful uppercut. We finally see the man's face: SHO'NUFF, THE SHOGUN OF HARLEM, stands tall as he looks at the group of gangsters.

He shouts, "Who's the Master?" The gangsters shout back, "Sho'nuff!" A group of girls walk behind Sho'nuff and help him to put on his red gear and sunglasses. He shouts, "Who's the Master?" We hear prisoners from their jail cells shouting, "SHO'NUFF". Sho'nuff calls out: "LEROY! The Shogun's coming for you!" We continue to hear the SHO-NUFF CHANT as Sho'nuff hops in a town car and drives off.

ACKNOWLEDGEMENTS

I would like to say thank you -

To Bruce Lee and Muhammad Ali for being my inspiration for it all.

To my friends and colleagues who provided many of the pictures for this book.

To Danny MacDonald my collaborator on the The Last Dragon: Guardians of the Glow, for agreeing to include the treatment within these pages.

To Joel Eisenberg for introducing me to my publisher.

To the many colleagues on screen, on stage and in the classroom who helped me grow as an actor and person.

To: my first Karate teacher, Gerald Orange; Ron Van Clief who helped make me ready for the streets of New York, they were tough back in the day; my friend Milton Lacroix for working my boxing skills to perfection; and to all my teachers who trained me over the years, pushing me to be better.

To my editor Matt who helped me get beyond my natural aversion to writing and pulled another 80 pages out of me!

To Judith Steele for her love and support.

To Ilka Scobie for her love and support.

To my brother, Meishan, for the great cover photo.

To Patricia Warren for her support and for helping me to organize my thoughts so I could get them out of my head and onto the page.

To Uncle Roy and his Wife Sarah for their love and support.

To my closest friends, you know who you are. Thank you for being there through it all.

Thank you to Sony Pictures Home Entertainment for the images on page 154 and 165

And finally, to you my fans, who have made this journey something special. I know we will see a lot more of each other.

Credits

This book is a work of art produced by Incorgnito Publishing Press.

Matthew Bucemi

Managing Editor

Patricia Warren

Associate Editor

Star Foos

Artist & Designer

Janice Bini

Chief Reader

Michael Conant

Publisher

Alysa Scanzano

Marketing Consultant

Marci Designs

Web Development

Graphic Production

Daria Lacy

March 2016

Incorgnito Publishing Press